Nature as well as the quality of his anthropomorphism.

Robbe-Grillet has, therefore, written novels, like *La Jalousie*, from which he, as author, appears to be absent (since he does not openly intrude to comment on the story as Hardy, Tolstoy, and so many traditional novelists would) but which, nevertheless, communicate his point of view. He is saying, in essence, that man must learn how to reject "tragedy."

Almost everything "seen" in a novel like *La Jalousie* depends on the particular selectivity of the protagonist's eye. Since Robbe-Grillet rejects analysis as an authorial intrusion, a protagonist's inner state of mind is not analyzed but "objectified" in terms of what he sees. This emphasis on the visible is what critics have now labeled "l'école du regard." Robbe-Grillet's contribution to the novel, therefore, consists in having masterfully combined Editorial Omniscience (the author's point of view) with Selective Omniscience (what the main character sees) in a simultaneous, unbroken, narrative technique—a new and important artistic achievement.

In writing the first book in English on Alain Robbe-Grillet, Ben F. Stoltzfus has made a valuable contribution to the understanding of a recent important phase of literature. Readers of the modern novel, as well as students of French literature and aesthetics, will find this work useful and informative.

BEN F. STOLTZFUS, a member of the Department of Romance Languages at the University of California at Riverside, has lived in Sofia, Istanbul, and Beirut and has studied in Paris —the last time in 1963–64 under a Fulbright Research Award. He has written extensively on modern French literature.

HARRY T. MOORE, general editor of this series, is Research Professor of English at Southern Illinois University and a reviewer of contemporary literature for the *New York Times*, *Saturday Review*, and other periodicals. Although best known for his books on D. H. Lawrence, he is also considered an authority on other modern writers.

CROSSCURRENTS *Modern Critiques*

CROSSCURRENTS / *Modern Critiques*
Harry T. Moore, *General Editor*

Ben F. Stoltzfus

Alain Robbe-Grillet

AND THE NEW FRENCH NOVEL

WITH A PREFACE BY
Harry T. Moore

Carbondale
SOUTHERN ILLINOIS UNIVERSITY PRESS

To Elizabeth

Copyright © 1964 by Southern Illinois University Press
All rights reserved
Library of Congress Catalog Card Number 64–10052
Printed in the United States of America
Designed by Andor Braun

IN WRITING the first book in English on Alain Robbe-Grillet, Ben F. Stoltzfus has made a valuable contribution to the understanding of a recent important phase of literature. Note that his subtitle promises something also about the new novel in general, of which Robbe-Grillet is a part. The book lives up to this promise, with its references to Nathalie Sarraute, Samuel Beckett, Michel Butor, and other members of the group generally thought of as writing the new novel, or nouveau roman.

The group indeed has various names as well as various aspects. It sometimes goes under the inclusive title of alittérature (or nonliterature), or of the école du regard (school of the look). It produces not only the nouveau roman but also what is called the antiroman (antinovel). Robbe-Grillet definitely belongs to the branch of the school which practices what is known as chosisme (thingism, or thingishness). This term suggests a concentration on material objects; as Robbe-Grillet has said, "things are there." He believes that literature has never even explored even their surfaces.

This movement, which began in the late 1940s, was from the first different from the dominant movements preceding it in French, the literature of existentialism and of the absurd. The antinovelists in their fiction and in their manifestoes advocated an escape from the traditional novel's preoccupation with straight-line plot, psychological analysis, and moral involvements.

These doctrines, and the novels (or antinovels) projecting them, appeared at a time when literature all over the
world had become too abstract and bodiless. Some authors
of the immediate past had written prose that had the
concreteness of the actual—James Joyce, D. H. Lawrence,
Marcel Proust, say—but their kind of writing no longer
appeared. Novels and stories sometimes contained descriptions, of the conventionally realistic kind—as in the cata-
loguing of properties in a room where the action was
taking place—but objects merely listed don't have the
solidity, the color, the vitality of objects as presented in
the writings of the older authors mentioned above or in
those of a Robbe-Grillet. Traditional novelists too often
fail to convey the effect that life makes upon the human
consciousness: their works have no chairs that the characters can really sit in, and no windows looking out on trees
that are fleshed in green, with sunlight rich on their
shaking leaves.

The chosistes, if they have done nothing else, have re-
stored a sense of concreteness to fiction. Their exclusion
of various other elements of the novel has been questioned,
as well as the manipulation of their technique, which is
not invariably successful; but at least the chosistes have
made readers once more aware that they step daily through
a world of solid objects, of glowing colors, of vital movement. The chosistes have done even more than this, for
even in their failures they have made their material seem
exciting, if only in showing how important a part of our
existence the physical objects of life are.

This doesn't mean that the chosistes necessarily "humanize" objects. Robbe-Grillet particularly avoids such
effects as those which Ruskin selected for examples of
what he called "the pathetic fallacy," such as "the cruel,
crawling foam" or "Now sleeps the crimson petal, now
the white." In order to escape from these anthropomorphic
reductions of experience, Robbe-Grillet, the former agron-
omist, projects his stories with an unemotional, geometric
precision as he measures landscapes and objects with com-
passes and calipers.

He tries to avoid metaphor, but this is strictly impossible; a writer can only diminish the use of metaphor. In the last of the novels dealt with in this study, for example —Dans le labyrinthe—the snow is described as "un peu plus tassé seulement," which in English translation becomes "a little more solidly packed"; and that is certainly a metaphorical idea (this would apply also to the usual meaning of the verb tasser, to heap). Incidentally, that same snow "a cessé a tomber"—"had ceased to fall." And the soldier in the snow-packed city is described as being "au pied de son réverbère—"at the foot of his streetlamp." This is a metaphor even if it is only, because it has become commonplace, what is called in English a dead metaphor. I am merely trying to point out that Robbe-Grillet can't escape figurative language altogether, though admittedly he does avoid sweeping use of it. Similarly, however he may strive to avoid meaning in the usual sense, he can't altogether do so, for even in his still-life approaches, the very objects that he chooses to present suggest a meaning. Why are these particular things projected, and why are they arranged in a certain pattern? By implication, Robbe-Grillet is making a statement about life—his very technique does that, of itself—and so he is indulging in philosophy, which deals in meaning. Yet in the commonest use of that word—what does such-and-such mean?— Robbe-Grillet is evading the concept, as his characters and situations are left in the mist; unless the reader has some idea as to what happened, he can't properly evaluate the meaning of the story itself. And with Robbe-Grillet the reader never really knows; the deaths, even murders, of certain characters may not be deaths at all, but fantasies. So here we have a special philosophy ("life exists in terms of objects"; "the events of life are a puzzle") and yet no meaning in the accepted sense, as found in the usual story.

Robbe-Grillet's first novel, Les Gommes, is at one level a parody of the roman policier and, at another, a commentary-by-parallel on a classic story, Oedipus the King. A detective, a politician, and a gangster are important figures in the book. Robbe-Grillet had not yet learned how to avoid symbols (the novel came out in 1953), for even the erasers of the title may be symbols, however parodically so, as in the case of the proprietor of a bistro, reflected in its mirrors, who suggests a fish in an aquarium. This is both symbol and metaphor, and there is even metaphor in the eraser the detective asks for at the store: "une gomme très douce," an eraser that is "sweet" (or "gentle"). But for the most part the story foreshadows Robbe-Grillet's later manner. The townscapes are done in a firm geometry. And the mystery here, often comic, is the mystery of events so often found in the author's later work.

My own favorite among his books is his second novel, Le Voyeur, published two years after Les Gommes. It might be said that by the time Robbe-Grillet wrote this second book, he had (and, printer, please leave all the words to follow as just separate words) every thing under control.

In this story, Mathias, a watch salesman, briefly revisits the island of his childhood, and while he is there a young girl is raped and murdered—or is she? Mathias, whose consciousness the reader becomes acquainted with as the watch salesman makes the short journey to the island by boat, is obsessed with young girls, with pieces of string, and with the flying gulls he keeps watching. He might be the murderer: if there was a murder. The story is a puzzle, but it is one which closely involves the reader because what happens in it happens intensively, through the slow, sure, repetitious projection of things upon the consciousness. Mathias's temperament gives at least one clue to the title, for psychosexually he is the voyeur, the scoptophile, the girl watcher, especially the watcher of little girls. And the timepieces Mathias sells emphasize the time element in the story, continually noted as in the roman-policier type of book once more being parodied. When Mathias, after three days on the island, boards the boat again, it is "four-fifteen exactly." The last object described in the book is a floating buoy, precisely rendered in terms of its vertical and horizontal lines. But its substructure, below the water, is a mélange of dancing shapes, suggesting the fluidity of the mystery.

In La Jalousie (1957), Robbe-Grillet carries to its extreme his technique of imposing lines, planes, cylinders, and ovals upon the consciousness of the reader as they are imposed upon the minds of the people in the story, which is set in a banana plantation. The narrative is not in the third person, and yet it is not exactly in the second person, either; everything is recorded through a detail-devouring eye; and there are snatches of dialogue. The reader can soon make his way into the maze of the book, and if he persists he will probably find the story—if story it is— fascinating. It is circular and full of repetitions; it is a tale told by a camera that continually roves back over the same objects and situations, or suggested situations; (as Mr. Stoltzfus notes, it is not like the suggested instrument in Christopher Isherwood's I Am a Camera). The reader may find that Robbe-Grillet's story of a triangle, and of fierce jealousy, has taken him through a reading experience more intense than he may find in many more comprehensible books.

Dans le labyrinthe (1959), already mentioned and quoted from, is another mystery, this time with something of the flavor of a Franz Kafka story. The labyrinth of the title is partly the snow-filled city which is the setting; a soldier from a defeated army tries to find his way through it in order to deliver a comrade's package. The messenger doesn't know what is in this cardboard box—some trivial letters—but he has promised the other soldier to carry it to a relative in the city. Wounded and exhausted as he goes through the snow-choked streets, the messenger continually meets a mysterious little boy and is continually haunted by a streetlamp whose cone of light is carefully demarcated. As in the case of Kafka, critics have tried to read into the messenger's quest an allegory of modern man, lost in civilization. But maybe Robbe-Grillet was only writing another chosiste story in which the death of the soldier—if he really does die—seems almost incidental in the white maze of baffling houses. (This author's latest novel, l'Immortelle, 1963, appeared too late to be discussed here.)

In the present study of Robbe-Grillet, Mr. Stoltzfus, who teaches at the University of California, Riverside, deals with all these matters far more fully, and also takes up Robbe-Grillet's 1961 film, l'Anée dernière à Marienbad (Last Year at Marienbad), as well as this author's various essays about his literary philosophy. Mr. Stoltzfus's text doesn't always gibe with some of the things said in this Preface—for example, he assumes the reality of the murder in Le Voyeur. He makes out a good case for his point of view, summing up the opinions of various critics in relation to the incident (or non-incident). Indeed, here and elsewhere he had scrupulously examined these none-too-easily-readable books of Robbe-Grillet and has provided some highly valuable insights into the author's method and his use of object and event. Altogether, Mr. Stoltzfus has made one of the most useful investigations of one of the most exciting movements in the area of the modern novel.

HARRY T. MOORE

Southern Illinois University
August 27, 1963

ACKNOWLEDGMENTS

IN ITS INCEPTION and preparation, this book owes much to the helpful suggestions, the assistance, and the advice of Professor Marshall Van Deusen, Professor and Mrs. Judd Hubert, Professor Fredrick Hoffman, and my wife.

Part of the material appeared in somewhat different form as "A Novel of Objective Subjectivity . . ." in *PMLA*, LXXVII (1962), 499–508. Related essays have appeared in *MLN* ("Alain Robbe-Grillet and Surrealism") and *La Revue des Lettres Modernes* ("La Connivence tragique de l'*Etranger* et du *Voyeur*").

CONTENTS

INTRODUCTION

THE PURPOSE of this book is threefold. First, to show how Robbe-Grillet's works evolve logically from one of the mainstreams of the western literary tradition; second, to evaluate in what way his novels contribute to and differ from this tradition; and third, to define a new concept of tragedy and to show how and why Robbe-Grillet's books represent, as Malraux phrased it *à propos* of *Sanctuary*, "the intrusion of Greek tragedy in the detective story."

Les Gommes (*The Gum Erasers*), *Le Voyeur* (*The Voyeur*), *La Jalousie* (*Jealousy*), and *L'Année dernière à Marienbad* (*Last Year at Marienbad*) demonstrate how man's tendency to anthropomorphize his environment can lead to tragedy. "Tragic complicity"—man's inability to accept the "distance" between his animate self and inanimate objects—leads him to humanize Nature and then incorporate it within himself. This anthropocentrism establishes a vicious circle—a man projects his feelings, emotions and passions onto and into things which, in turn, and once so "contaminated," are capable of precipitating a corresponding reaction in him, the perceiver. Thus Mathias, a sex pervert and the main character of *Le Voyeur*, "contaminates" a cigarette wrapper, a rusty piton, a piece of string, figure eight patterns, and these objects, once "contaminated" with his particular emotional disturbance, as projections of and catalysts for his sexuality, lead him to and provoke the murder of a thirteen-year-old girl. In *La Jalousie* a centipede is the objective correlative and eventually the symbol of the husband's jealousy. Each time the husband sees, imagines, or remembers a centipede (or its stain), the animal (or its image) precipitates a jealous crisis. A similar involvement with objects and things of his environment will lead Wallas, the protagonist of *Les Gommes*, to shoot his father because he has not resolved an Oedipus complex. Who would believe that the lovely heroine of *L'Année dernière à Marienbad* could be seduced by X in the formal, geometric gardens of a luxurious baroque château? Yet her "persuasion," as Robbe-Grillet calls it, depends on the anthropomorphosis of objects (such as a picture or a bracelet) allegedly exchanged "last year" at Marienbad.

Dans le labyrinthe (*In the Labyrinth*) and *Instantanés* (*Snapshots*) are departures from the conditioned reflex pattern of objects influencing behavior. The interminably long, detailed, geometric descriptions of things—Robbe-Grillet's novelistic trademark—are still present, but they no longer necessarily demonstrate the fallacy of "tragic complicity." Their purpose now is to reveal the creative possibilities extant in the interaction of imagination and environment. The artist, therefore, may consciously "contaminate" objects, or nature, in order to communicate a meaningful experience about the human predicament. *Dans le labyrinthe*, as the title suggests, is a statement about man's situation, and the novel implies that, until our civilization can produce one or more young Theseuses, capable of slaying the Minotaur and of rejecting "tragedy," man will remain the victim of the nightmare of history—war.

Robbe-Grillet's narrative technique, which focuses on a description of objects in space, has frequently provoked hostility and incomprehension in readers and critics. Abstract, geometric descriptions, however, represent an oblique authorial intrusion into a narrative from which the author seems to have been refined out of existence. The intent of geometric and arithmetic descriptions, then, is to communicate distance—that necessary "distance" between man and Nature—whereas the more conventional descriptions (there are gradations) are to communicate the type and intensity of a particular character's "complicity." Robbe-Grillet has, therefore, written novels from which he, as an author, appears to be absent (insomuch as he does not openly intrude to comment on the story as so many traditional novelists would) but which, nevertheless, communicate his point of view. Almost everything "seen" in the novel depends on the particular selectivity of the protagonist's eye. This selectivity communicates his psychological state of mind which is not analysed—Robbe-Grillet rejects this kind of authorial intrusion—but seen. Robbe-Grillet has, therefore, masterfully combined Editorial Omniscience (the author's oblique comment) and Selective Omniscience (what the main character sees) into one simultaneous narrative technique—a new and important artistic achievement.

BEN F. STOLTZFUS

15 March 1963
University of California
Riverside

Alain Robbe-Grillet

AND THE NEW FRENCH NOVEL

1   NEW FORMS FOR OLD

A NEW LITERARY SCHOOL has arisen in Paris since the early 1950's. The authors of the "nouveau roman" have attracted almost immediate and world-wide attention due to their technical audacity and the forcefulness of their manifestoes. The event is not unimportant. With the exception of Surrealism in 1924 and Existentialism after 1945 France has not witnessed, in this century, the emergence of a group of writers with comparable vigor, ability, perhaps genius, and who, in spite of inevitable and profound differences, have in common a fundamental determination, in their search for new artistic forms, new relationships, and new meanings, *not* to imitate the traditional novel.

These new novelists, Samuel Beckett, Nathalie Sarraute (though obviously Beckett and Sarraute cannot be described as new), Alain Robbe-Grillet, Claude Simon, Michel Butor, and others have pushed the domain of the novel beyond the experimental frontiers of Proust, Joyce, James, or Faulkner. The moral, perhaps even metaphysical, climate of these writers obviates the existential despair of Malraux, Sartre, and Camus. If these writers are "engagés," they are committed, as Robbe-Grillet states in an article in *La Revue de Paris* (September, 1961), not to action, as were their immediate predecessors, but to literature. Their preoccupations are neither political nor humanitarian. This does not mean that "man" has been banished from their novels as many critics affirm. On the contrary, man has, as Robbe-Grillet insists, been given first place, and the subjective role of the reader has perhaps become greater than it ever was in the past.

In the same way that the movies have stressed the restriction of the angle of vision, the new novel has evolved a new perspective and limitation of the point of view. Robbe-Grillet particularly, like the movie director, is asking questions such as: from where is this object seen? At what angle is it seen? At what distance? With what kind of lighting? Does the viewer linger on the object or does he pass over it quickly? Is the viewer moving or is he stationary? The new novelist is no longer omniscient as Sartre succinctly phrases it in his attack on Mauriac in *Situations*. "It is no longer God who describes the world, it is man, *one* man. Even if it is not a personage, it is in any case *a human eye*." [1]

In Beckett's famous trilogy (*Molloy, Malone Dies, The Unnamable*) the omniscient author has vanished and in his place we have only the consciousness of a personage who communicates obliquely. In Beckett's novels, as Hoffman in his book on Samuel Beckett points out, we have "conscious selves maneuvering through spaces occupied by objects that are either testimonies of or challenges to them"; but most specifically we witness the interior monologue of "interior selves" who are communicating a very specific and limited point of view. These preoccupations seem to represent a new philosophical conditioning of literature whereby the author's disappearance suggests a diminished structural confidence and a decline in shared metaphysical values. Beckett's characters, forever crippled or losing limbs, are deeply suspicious of a God who has created them as defective creatures.[2] Malone, in *Malone Dies*, like Stephen, in Joyce's *Portrait*, becomes the creator of a fiction. Thus we have Beckett creating Malone and Malone in turn engendering other personages within the novel in the same manner that Stephen, having denied the formal requisites of a Creator, becomes in himself a creator. A *Portrait of the Artist as a Young Man* contains both the formula and the direction for the most significant trend in the technical development of twentieth-century fiction—the abolition of the omniscient author.[3]

The new novelists speak of the complexity of the modern world and of the impossibility for any one man to preside in omniscient judgment on the destinies of his protagonists. Thus the Victorian novel and the world of Balzac, they say, are dead and the author as an all-seeing God has disappeared. It is impossible, says Michel Butor (though he himself does not reject Balzac as completely as do Sarraute and Robbe-Grillet) in "Le Roman comme recherche" ("The Novel as a Quest"),[4] to assimilate all the information which constantly bombards our senses. The novelist must therefore find a new artistic form whose power of integration is stronger than ever before.

Robbe-Grillet singles out Balzac as being typical of the omnipresent, all-seeing, all-knowing author who anticipates every thought and action of his characters, comments on their behavior, and describes the scene, not through the eyes of a single protagonist, but from top, bottom, side, and inside, in one simultaneous all-englobing vision. Nathalie Sarraute in her collection of essays entitled *L'Ere du soupçon*,[5] says that Balzac's novels are "suspect," because his convention of representing fictional reality no longer convinces, because no one man is endowed with such all-seeing power. The modern intelligent reader, insists Sarraute, doubts the authenticity and veracity of this omniscience. He has read Joyce, Proust, and Freud and he is impatient with what Sarraute claims is the arbitrary nature of plot and characterization. The new novelists, she says, are not interested in creating types like Mme Bovary, le Père Goriot, or Julien Sorel because, on the one hand, they do not want to repeat what has already been done and, on the other, because both the novelist and the reader no longer believe in the verisimilitude of such creations. She has therefore entirely eliminated plot and characterization from her novels.

Much of Sarraute's theoretical writing is polemical and corresponds, no doubt, to what Malcolm Cowley describes as the "ritual burial" of past writers by the emerging younger generation which must attract attention to itself. Obviously Sarraute is forcing the issue when she asks if there is a story which, for authenticity and reader interest, can compare with true life accounts of concentration camps or the battle of Stalingrad. The novelist has perhaps never aimed at being "believed" in the way that we credit the "authenticity" or "true life accounts" of real events. Every artistic convention is "synthetic," even Sarraute's dialogues. What she means, I suppose, is that the typical artistic conventions of the nineteenth-century novel are outmoded. It is the deliberate and obvious author intrusion of the traditional novel which destroys the illusion of truth he is trying to communicate. The new novelists argue, therefore, that three of the yardsticks by which the success of the traditional novel was measured (plot, characterization, and Editorial Omniscience) are now passé and that the modern artist must find new means—new artistic conventions—to communicate his particular vision. In order to accomplish this, Sarraute has eliminated the tell-tale "he said," or "she answered," as dialogue indicators. Such directives, she says, are an unnecessary intrusion by the author and inhibit the desirable rapport between the reader, the relationships being presented to him, and the artistic experience. This is why her transitions from conversation to subconversation, or from one personage to another, are presented simply by shifts in punctuation.

One of the most striking changes that has taken place between conventional fiction and modern fiction, as Friedman points out,[6] is that today the fictional event itself dominates rather than the overt attitude of the narrator. Friedman characterizes the fictional event as direct and immediate and editorial comment as necessarily second-hand and indirect. With Editorial Omniscience the tendency is away from scene towards an authorial voice which dominates the material. In *Tom Jones* and *War and Peace*, for instance, Fielding and Tolstoy have interpolated their essays as separate detachable chapters within the body of the work while Hardy chooses to comment in the midst of the action itself. These authors not only report what goes on in the minds of their characters but they also criticize their reactions. Hardy, for instance, depicts Tess wandering about the countryside after her calamitous encounter with Alex, imagining natural sights and sounds as proclaiming her guilt. Then he deliberately informs the reader that she is wrong in feeling this way: "But this encompassment of her own characterization, based upon shreds of convention, peopled by phantoms and voices antipathetic to her, was a sorry and mistaken creation of Tess's fancy—a cloud of moral hobgoblins by which she was terrified without reason" (end of Ch. XIII).

The important distinction then between the "nouveau roman" and traditional novelists like Fielding, Tolstoy, Hardy, or Balzac is that the latter overtly interpret the novel for the reader, whereas the judgment contained within the new novel is covert. The initial reaction to the "nouveau roman" and the absence of Editorial Omniscience, particularly to the novels of Simon, Sarraute, and Robbe-Grillet, was one of almost total incomprehension. But incomprehension, even hostility, no longer surprise us. Artistic innovations have always encountered resistance until the new conventions have been assimilated. Thus the immediate impression we get from reading Robbe-Grillet's novels is that he does not judge his characters. Nothing could be farther from the truth however, as, I hope, will become evident throughout this book. The fundamental distinction between Robbe-Grillet's technique and the example I have just given from Hardy is that whereas both authors judge their characters, Robbe-Grillet's judgment is hidden, oblique, an inherent function of form. Tess is anthropomorphizing the world around her as much as Robbe-Grillet's characters do or as does Meursault in *L'Etranger* before he shoots the Arab. Camus and Robbe-Grillet, unlike Hardy, however, do not intrude to explain what is happening to their heroes. This has become the reader's function. And this explains why the role of the reader is now more difficult. Today the reader must decipher the moral but he cannot do this unless he understands the new function of technique.

Robbe-Grillet has been criticized for his undue preoccupation with technique whereas, in fact, such preoccupation was necessary if he was to evolve a new artistic form. The modern novelist is, in a way, as omniscient as he was before. He only appears to be absent. It is this "deception" which, for its success, will depend on the artistic fusion of form and content. *L'Etranger*, *La Jalousie*, and *Le Planétarium* reveal how far the modern novel has progressed as an art form. If the fusion of form (how the moral is said) and content (what the moral intent is) is the ultimate goal of the artistic process, then the "nouveau roman" has created works of art of singular distinction and beauty.

It is this "fusion" which makes them, at least for the present, difficult to read. The modern reader has not yet adjusted to the absence of authorial intrusion or to what appears like absence. The reader's role will consist in giving the new novel meaning as he follows unexplained signposts which are there to guide him. It is the discrepancy between Robbe-Grillet's geometric descriptions with descriptions of color and texture and movement which provides us with one of the essential clues to his particular brand of Selective Omniscience—that is, a world seen through the eyes of one protagonist.

Henry James who, like Sarraute, wanted to eliminate the irresponsible illusion-breaking garrulousness of the omniscient author looked upon the arbitrary and unconsidered shift in point of view as a menace to the intimacy and illusion of truth. James substituted the consciousness of one or more personages for the all-seeing and all-knowing author and it is this or these states of consciousness which, respectively, filter the action. Robbe-Grillet suggests that this is the most significant trend in fiction of our century. His own novels, as we shall see presently, represent a unique and original elaboration of this tendency. James, in his 1907–9 prefaces, writes of finding a "centre" or "focus" for his stories through which to frame the narrative, action, and plot within the consciousness of a protagonist, while critics like Beach, Lubbock, Tate, Schorer, and Friedman believe that the modern novelist wants the story to tell itself and in order to accomplish this a limitation in the point of view is indispensable.[7]

ii

Nathalie Sarraute has given us novels (*Tropismes, Portrait d'un inconnu, Martereau, le Planétarium*) which embody the characteristics she refers to in her critical writings. She blends the traditional form of dialogue with a "sous-conversation" (sub-conversation) destined to capture the gropings or "tropisms" that may exist and be dimly sensed in the subconversational world of inner monologues which are registered as vague premonitions long before feelings are rendered conscious in speech form. Sartre, in his preface to her *Portrait of Somebody Unknown*, describes this as a "protoplasmic vision of our interior world." In *The Age of Suspicion* Sarraute describes these subterranean or submarine regions of consciousness as peopled with shy timid creatures like bugs, leeches, or snails which hide in the shadows and are afraid of light. It is the "protoplasmic" movements of our subconscious which interest her and which for her represent the true domain of the novelist's art. Beneath the surface of inevitably conventional situations, such as a family quarrel over money or the problems of finding and furnishing an apartment, violent conflicts are in progress. These inner dramas are made up of "attacks, triumphs, retreats, defeats, caresses, bites, rapes, murders, generous abandons, or humble submissions." Her novels go beyond the dialogues of Ivy Compton-Burnett to reveal dimensions of the mind which even Proust did not describe.

Sarraute has devised an ingenious system of punctuation to alert the reader to abrupt and unannounced shifts and transitions from conversation to subconversation within the consciousness of different protagonists. Plot for her is inconsequential since what interests her is not what happens, but the subtle interrelationships between people. This is, again, the domain of Ivy Compton-Burnett. Sarraute, however, in exploring the slimy recesses of our subconscious, likes to observe and finger the scurrying activities of her animal progeny and, after long and detailed exploration of these shadowy regions, the statements of her protagonists assume new and varied nuances of meaning.

Robbe-Grillet's novels, though they might seem antipodal to Sarraute's, also reveal an extreme fascination and preoccupation with the workings of the mind and the subconscious. Whereas Sarraute's inner monologue is an extension of Joyce or Proust, Robbe-Grillet's "objectivity" descends in direct line from Flaubert. But Robbe-Grillet carries the technique of minute and detailed visual description of objects beyond anything envisioned by any other writer. Even though superficially this technique of the visual (*l'école du regard* or *chosisme*) would seem to negate any concern with depth psychology (as the hasty pronouncements of some critics indicated), it does in fact project the subconscious onto these objects. This is done in two ways: first of all in terms of the selectivity of the protagonist (the tendency to perceive what is most meaningful to a particular state of mind), and secondly in terms of the objective correlatives which the author manipulates in order to reveal the state of mind of the protagonist. Thus Robbe-Grillet in *Le Voyeur* will describe bits of string, a rusty piton, figure eight shapes, and a very young girl as seen through the eyes of the watch salesman, Mathias. These apparently unconnected objects will, in the course of the novel, reveal Mathias' sexuality and the nature of his crime. This Selective Omniscience, at times, verges on Editorial Omniscience whenever Robbe-Grillet describes landscape, not as a function of perception, but as something *there*. Whenever this occurs, the description is never arbitrary, it is always there for Mathias, and the movement of the ocean, as an objective correlative, and in the light of previous associations, functions as the analogue of Mathias' subconscious: the mounting violence of the ocean will correspond to the mounting violence of his sexuality. Though Robbe-Grillet's novels seem to be devoid of psychological depth in the literary sense, they possess as much depth of meaning as do Sarraute's.

Both authors refer to the extreme subjectivity of their personages. Sarraute uses interior monologue and conversation, Robbe-Grillet uses virtually no conversation and relies entirely for his effect on a visual description of the external world. With Robbe-Grillet there remains the durable image of *things*. With Sarraute the reader is left with a "néant," an impalpable "malaise," the nothing of a consciousness which is not aware of external objects but of an internal state of mind. The rapidity, the complexity, and the minuteness of Sarraute's almost invisible dramas, the dialogues themselves which shimmer like light on water, fade with the progression and the elaboration of emotion into relationships which are almost too ephemeral to grasp (since she emphasizes the secret and uncertain interior universe and minimizes the misleading signs of appearances) and are lost, as they are in life, under the conventional surface-play of things, habit, stereotype, and time.

Robbe-Grillet traces the inner psychological world of his protagonists as it registers on environmental objects and stimuli. Here is manifest on Robbe-Grillet, though not on Sarraute, the influence of the movies. Sarraute feels that the novel's strength depends on dialogue because only through dialogue can the gropings and conflicts of the subconversational world be revealed. It is these subtle interrelationships, she feels, which the movies cannot capture. Her novels, like Ivy Compton-Burnett's, verge on the pure dialogue of the theater. Robbe-Grillet's novels, on the other hand, due to his particular "objective" technique have evolved naturally towards the movies as an art form. This explains why the film script for *Last Year at Marienbad* reads like a novel. Flashbacks in his novels have the same function and are described in the same way that a flashback occurs on the screen: it is seen in the *present* and the viewer or reader reacts to the film on the screen or to the "inner film" of the protagonist's memory (when it is being described) as though it were happening now rather than in the past or in an imaginary future. The identity or technique between *Last Year at Marienbad* and his novels is evident. This emphasis on events occurring in the present is, along with the limitation of the point of view, the most interesting phenomenon of the "new novel." These two factors seem to require unprecedented reader participation because the dislocation of narrative sequence in time-space (memory, present reality, future fantasy or projected reality), in terms of a continuous present, is not always easy to follow or anticipate. The reader must contribute actively to the elaboration and metamorphosis of thought and emotion. The fact that everything is happening in the present, which the reader is actively interpreting, gives the narrative an immediacy and impact absent from the traditional past tense story. The use of the past tense and the editorial intrusion of Hardy create a "distance" between the reader and the novel. The new novelists have tried to reduce this "distance" by eliminating as many *evident* author interferences as possible. Such evident intrusions, argues Sarraute, destroy the true intensity of the artistic impact.

Claude Simon's use of the present participle in such novels as *l'Herbe* (*The Grass*) or *le Vent* (*The Wind*) is designed to communicate the same ephemeral intensity of events occurring in the ever fluid present. Michel Butor's use of the second person pronoun *vous*, instead of the first person narrative *I* or the third person narrative, in *La Modification* (*A Change of Heart*) reveals similar if not identical preoccupations: to reduce the traditional distance between protagonist and reader, and in so doing, to involve the reader in the search or quest for meaning and identity. Thus, the importance and interest of *La Modification* reside not in the fact that the protagonist will or will not leave his wife for his mistress, but in the evolution of the husband's thinking which will explain his "change of heart." This *vous* (though perhaps artifical and not entirely successful) is meant to involve the reader-protagonist in the ramifications of thought, dream, rationalization, flashback, memory, and anticipation, in an "organic" twenty-four hour sequence as it unfolds with the ticking of every railroad mile from Paris to Rome.

In another of Butor's novels, *l'Emploi du temps* (translatable as *Time Table* or *Schedule* or *Use of Time*), Jacques Revel's reconstruction of what happened to him, a foreigner in the English city of Bleston, vividly recalls the wandering search of Joyce's heroes through Dublin. The first person journal-type narrative (reminiscent of Sartre's *Nausea*) is designed to unravel the labyrinthine meaning of events which, in the course of a year, are responsible for the protagonist's feeling of confusion and derangement. The novel does not follow the chronology of events as they occurred. The journal traces, instead, an inner psychic chronology of time-space as Jacques Revel tries to determine whether he is or is not responsible for someone's attempted assassination. This work, which derives so closely from Robbe-Grillet's first published (1953) novel, *Les Gommes* (*The Gum Erasers*), stresses another basic goal of these writers—to communicate the idea of a quest or search. In this sense, *Les Gommes* and *l'Emploi du temps* are both neo-detective novels.

This notion of quest does not stem only from the detective novel. Olivier de Magny rightly observes that Faulkner, in writing *Absalom, Absolom!*, has set a precedent for creating a novel which questions its own existence.[8] Quentin and Shreve are asked to reconstruct the past and to attribute, and hence create, possible character motivation in the light of certain occurrences. The novel fulfills itself at the same time that its author seeks the meaning for and tries to reveal the reality of the South or its decadence in the light of fratricide or civil war. Thus Faulkner seems to initiate what Butor calls "le roman comme recherche." The true novel, says Butor, allows the reader to rediscover a pattern of events which are the reflection of his own inner life. A novelist like Simon will therefore prefer the present tense because it communicates the immediacy of experience, not as a past event, but as occurring now.

An event which is described in the past is subject to

distortion and bias of memory and is therefore "suspect." Since the reader is being asked to judge for himself, without the author commentary reminiscent of Hardy or of Balzac, the present tense becomes the logical narrative choice. Thus, in Simon's *Le Palace* (1962) time and memory have disappeared. *La Route des Flandres* (1960, *Flanders' Road*) gave the reader the impression of time as a flowing river moving from the past through the present into the future. *Le Palace*, on the contrary, is static, and Simon has tried, more scrupulously than ever before, to render sensorially the impact of an event or events as present experience. Even the recollection of an assassination takes on a density of meaning full of a strange oneiric simultaneity. The assassination itself lasts only a few seconds. But the remembrance of it assumes, in the narrator's memory and hence in the reader's imagination, a duration which is more meaningful than the original event. Fragments of the Spanish Civil War are narrated to an observer (the reader) by an Italian, a teacher, and an American, thus giving the epigraph of the novel an ambiguous intensity: "Revolution: the movement of a mobile which, in traversing the distance of a closed curve, passes repeatedly and successively over the same points."

Simon attempts to capture an inexhaustible reality by putting together traits and accumulating parentheses with each detail added to the previous ones and without any one of them being erased. He has almost eliminated punctuation. His sentences run together for pages and pages with all manner of complex and elliptical references. The profusion of such references and the complexity of sentence structure, like grass growing, or the blowing of the wind, are to reproduce, even be, the multiplicity and ambiguity of life. Time is dislocated—past, present, and future blend and overlap (as they do in Robbe-Grillet) in a manner designed to capture not clock chronology, but the inner time sequence of a living being. His novels are a searching attempt at re-learning to see the world. In *L'Herbe* he has tried to grasp and reconstruct not only the passing of time in its irregular flow, but the immediacy of experience which is not linear but voluminous, hence the epigraph: "No one person makes the story, you cannot see it, any more than you can see the grass grow." As Jacques Guicharnaud rightly observes, in his article on Claude Simon ("Remembrance of Things Passing"),[9] the present participles of Simon's novels are the blades of grass, transparent and indeterminate, which grow and proliferate and which are replaced by others and still others. Simon finally communicates the abundance and richness and overflowingness of living experience in the *present*. His style then is one of the solutions to the problem originally stated by Sartre and which has been a constant concern to French novelists, namely to capture the intensity and overwhelming ambiguity of the present.

These are the trends of the "new novel." The "new novelists" are, in no small measure, Sartre's offspring. Nurtured on existentialism and Hüsserlian phenomenology, these writers have evolved beyond the novel as theory, which is at the same time Sartre's contribution and his weakness, and have written novels which Sartre would have wished to write but never could. He is a great precursor and a great theorist but he lacks the talent of his progeny. They have written books which are the fruition of existential theory and yet in which a doctrinaire self-consciousness is absent. This does not mean that these are not self-conscious works of art. On the contrary. The "new novel," as an art form (see Daniel Castelain's book *Une Rencontre improbable* 1961, *An Improbable Encounter*), reveals an extreme self-consciousness. Sartre's theorizing and James's concern for point of view have been thoroughly assimilated into an indistinguishable blend of form and content. This is, I suppose, or should be, the goal of every artist. Thus Robbe-Grillet can write what seem to be "technique" novels and at the same time make a significant statement about the human situation. His novels are not pure form, as many critics affirm, but the perfect artistic fusion of content and meaning which is its form. This is no small achievement and I would venture to say that Robbe-Grillet is one of the most important French novelists since Camus.

IN AN ARTICLE in the *NNRF* ("Nature, Humanisme, Tragédie," Oct. 1958) Alain Robbe-Grillet states that Albert Camus, as "everyone knows, has designated as *absurdity* the impassable abyss that stands between man and the world, between the aspirations of the human spirit and the incapacity of the world to satisfy them." The "absurd" is therefore for Camus neither in man nor in things, but in the "impossibility of establishing between the two any *rapport* other than 'strangeness.'"

Robbe-Grillet goes on to say that Meursault, the protagonist of *L'Etranger*, engages in a kind of bitter and fascinated connivance with the world, whose "absurdity" leads to disappointment, withdrawal, and finally revolt. He concludes that *things* draw the protagonist into his criminal act; that the sun, the sea, the dazzling sand, and the glistening knife, are involved in a certain complicity. It is the specific manner in which Meursault humanizes the world about him which Robbe-Grillet seems to object to; that in spite of Meursault's apparent indifference to and alienation from his environment, Camus has used metaphors in such a way as to negate this alienation:

> The countryside is "gorged with sunlight," the evening is "like a melancholy truce," the holes in the roadway reveal the "shining flesh" of the tar, the earth is "blood colored," the sunlight is a "dazzling rain," its reflection on a shell is a "sword of light," the day has "cast anchor in an ocean of boiling metal." . . . Not to mention the "breathing"

of the "lazy" waves, the "sleeping" promontory, the "panting" sea and the "cymbals" of the sun.

The focal scene of the novel, the one in which Meursault shoots the Arab, then becomes the perfect image of what Robbe-Grillet calls a "painful solidarity." The implacable sun which is reflected on the knife blade held by the Arab "strikes" Meursault on the forehead and "grinds" into his eyes. His hand clenches the revolver as he tries to "shake" the sun and the four successive revolver shots are like four sharp raps on the door of misfortune. Robbe-Grillet calls this "absurdity" a form of "tragic Humanism." For, instead of recognizing the separation of man and the world, as the postulation of the "absurd" implies, it re-emphasizes his solidarity with it. Tragedy, says Robbe-Grillet, is man's attempt to "recuperate" the separation between himself and things; to make of this distance a new value. Man's greatest dignity, following the premise of this "recuperation," is to sing of his own obliteration by time and death. This "chant sacré," as Malraux calls it in *Les Voix du silence*, is the only means available to man by which he can challenge the forces of destiny. Tragedy, then, is a sort of contest in which victory arises from defeat. This "tragic Humanism" which will allow nothing to escape from its domain insists therefore on a new form of solidarity in which the alienation between man and object leads to salvation. And so, in the final passage of the book, Meursault declares: "for the first time I confided in the tender indifference of the world. To feel it so much like me, so fraternal."

This complicity between Meursault and Nature, however, has a purpose, for it serves to emphasize not his alienation from Nature but his striking resemblance to it. Meursault is sentenced, not because he has shot an Arab, but because he has "buried his mother with the heart of a criminal." And the prosecuting attorney is no doubt right, for he is equating a "criminal heart" with "indifference" which is fundamentally Meursault's crime—his fraternal bond with the Universe. It is this indifference which the judge and a bourgeois society cannot tolerate, and Meursault will therefore be executed in the name of the "French people." Meursault, though he feels alienated from the world, is really in harmony with it. If he is a "stranger," it is not to Nature, but to the mores of society. He is therefore a "man of bad habits," as the prosecuting attorney is so fond of saying.

But Meursault's apparent alienation from the world about him is really a mask for the fact that beneath his superficial indifference lie the scars of a great deception. When his boss asks him to go to Paris and he refuses, he thinks about a time in the past when he used to be ambitious. This is obviously a value which he no longer shares with other people. And when, in answer to Marie's question, Meursault says that he could easily marry someone else, it does not mean that he dislikes her. He is simply playing for higher stakes. His love affair is not really with Marie but with the whole world. And insomuch as there are many Maries, within the context of his larger love-affair, he is being perfectly consistent. When did the disenchantment occur? Certainly before his mother's death, since his reaction to her passing away is already one of total indifference: "In the final analysis," he says, "nothing had changed."

We surmise, from the few clues that Meursault does give us in his narrative, that at some moment in the past he saw the meaning behind the "blinding light" of the sun; that at some particular moment before the narrative begins he came to the conclusion that he was living in an "absurd" Universe. His mother's death then merely accentuates an already too painful awareness—hence his apparent indifference which, psychologically speaking, is a defense mechanism of withdrawal. A painful stimulus in animals evokes a withdrawal response. And so with Meursault. But he is ambivalent. He loves the world and at the same time he resents the sun's symbolic slap in the face. This is the meaning of his "lover's quarrel," as Robbe-Grillet calls it. He wants to live in eternal harmony with the sun and the ocean and the beach and love, but he realizes, even before he informs us of the fact in his prison cell, that one day these things will be denied him. He wants the moon, as Caligula so nicely puts it, but the moon is out of reach of mortals.

Meursault's descendants are Caligula and Jan's sister (in *Le Malentendu*), both of whom have "seen the light" and who are acting out the logical consequences of their encounter with an "indifferent" world. Meursault's murder then is a manifestation of his revolt. But it is not a premeditated crime. Meursault's quarrel is not with the Arab. He is the unfortunate victim of a deception which staggers the imagination. Meursault is perfectly right, when questioned during the trial as to the motive of his assault, to blame the sun. For the sun, with all its symbolic overtones and associated meanings, is the force that "triggers" his revolver. The long sequence of anthropomorphic metaphors which Robbe-Grillet refers to, before the actual shooting, are the objectification of Meursault's great bond with Nature. He is alive and he senses that nature is also alive. His dark mood which Marie notices that same morning can only be a more acute and sudden awareness of his own contingency. And so, when he returns to the beach with the revolver, after the first fight, he is not looking for a quarrel with the Arab, since he is even surprised to see him, but with something which he can only vaguely grasp at, the sun. The sun does not disappoint him for it oppresses him with its heat, makes him perspire, and finally, when the light "splashes" on the Arab's knife and "strikes" him on the forehead with a liquid blade that "blinds" his eyes with a veil of sweat, the ocean and the sun seem to have combined forces in an effort to annihilate him: "It was then that everything wavered unsteadily. The sea's breath bore down with a heavy ardent mockery. It seemed to me the bottom of the sky was falling out in a sudden rain of fire. My whole being stiffened and my hand clenched the revolver." It is then that he pulls the trigger in an apparently involuntary effort to defend himself; and in so doing, he shoots the Arab. This explains his hesitation between the first shot and the next four. The first one was in self-defense, but once he realizes that the sun has tricked him again, all his anger surges forward and he vents his wrath against the Universe by pumping four additional shots into the inert corpse lying in front of him. The prosecuting attorney could not hope to understand the metaphysical implications motivating this senseless crime. He is enmeshed in his own religious doctrine and in the legal machinery of man-made justice. And so "everything is true and everything is false" as the defense attorney astutely says. Meursault does indeed seem to have "buried his mother with the heart of a criminal." But once we go behind the external facts of the narrative to the clues which Meursault gives us so sparingly in his first person monologue, and once we understand Camus' stylistic balance between symbol and reality and metaphor, we unlock the door to Meursault's unverbalized psychic life and we understand the motivation for his crime of "passion." Because of this unspoken level the reader must involve himself in the book, he must piece the clues together, he must decipher the relevance of detail, if he is to grasp its total meaning, artistically as well as symbolically. Otherwise, perhaps because the novel's first impact is primarily visceral, he only vaguely apprehends its import.

Le Voyeur is a novel about a watch salesman, Mathias, who returns to the island of his childhood in order to sell wrist watches to its inhabitants. In the course of events he sadistically murders a thirteen-year-old girl Jacqueline. The chronology of events is so dislocated that the reader is, at first, hopelessly caught in the labyrinth of a seemingly inexplicable sequence.

In this narrative Robbe-Grillet appears to carry the reader involvement one step further than Camus by eliminating all conscious thought on the part of his protagonist. But this is a deception and an illusion. The protagonist's eyes, by what they see (that is the objects they describe, select, and linger on) are the reader's picture window, not only to the travelling salesman's external reality, but to his inner psychic necessity. Everything that Mathias sees, the reader sees. The reader, like Mathias, must visualize every object and every event (real as well as those of memory and phantasy) and, if he does, if the reader puts all the pieces of this composite reality together, he has solved the riddle of the mind of a sex pervert. Though Robbe-Grillet's technique is different, in that he deliberately distorts clock chronology for the sake of the mind's dislocated chronology, the effect, that is the absence of author analysis and inner monologue, is the same as Camus'. Meursault in Part I tells us nothing of what is really going on inside his mind. We must infer this from his actions, his reactions to people and events, and the way he describes his environment. And so with Mathias: we must infer what he is thinking by what he sees and does and particularly by the way he distorts reality. This is our big clue to the fact that he is not normal. Gradually the image of murder appears on the screen of our imagination and we conclude from the evidence the author has given us that Mathias is associating past, present, and future in a constant now. Camus, through Meursault's narrative, has given the same kind of evidence, from which we conclude that he, Meursault, is fundamentally innocent. Nature, as Robbe-Grillet says, was an accomplice and an instigator. But just as Meursault bears the seed of his crime within him, so also does Mathias bear the seed of murder inside him. And in the same way that the heat, the sun, the sand, and the ocean lead Meursault to shoot the Arab, so also the piece of string, the blue cigarette wrapper, the rusty piton, the slap of the waves, the movie poster, the picture of Jacqueline, lead Mathias on the irrevocable path of possible rape and murder. Both men are victims of their environment but they are also men with drives. Meursault wants unlimited happiness and his crime is one of metaphysical revolt: what Balzac, in *La Peau de Chagrin*, calls the discrepancy between the *pouvoir* and the *vouloir*. Mathias' crime is the result of a sexual "perversion," the obsessive need to satisfy an immediate drive. But there is the suggestion in *Le Voyeur* that Mathias' crime stems from some kind of sexual repression and inhibition.

Mathias remembers being closed in his room as a boy where he drew a sedentary sea-gull on a phallic post. He also played "uncertain" but obviously sexual games with bits of string and sea anemones. In his adult life all but one of the sea-gulls are airborne, a fact which, in itself, seems to suggest a kind of freedom and release from inhibitions but, ironically enough, this freedom is an even greater prison, for he is trapped by the conditioned reflexes of his own sexuality.

It is the above-mentioned object-complicity which Robbe-Grillet denounces and yet, artistically speaking, imitates. Though in his own novels, he professes to refuse "tragedy" as he defines it, Camus' use of the anthropomorphic metaphor has given Robbe-Grillet essential information on the handling of form and content. In fact, one of the reasons so many bad articles have been written about Robbe-Grillet is that, in his early theoretical writings, his insistence on a pure objectivism misled critics to assume that his protagonists were not "passionately" involved in their environment, whereas Mathias, in *Le Voyeur*, and the unnamed husband in *La Jalousie* are the victims of "tragic complicity." The objects which surround them, though they appear to be described with the "objectivity" of a camera eye, are full of meaning—not symbolic meaning, for Robbe-Grillet would insist on the world's indifference to man. It is man who endows objects with meaning, and if strings, figure eights, rusty pitons, and centipedes have meaning, it is only in relation to the psychotic and deranged world of the protagonists who exist within the confines of the novel.

The most interesting aspect about Robbe-Grillet's *NNRF* article is that, while he appears to be rejecting the classical anthropomorphic metaphor which infuses the world of objects with human meaning and while he even seems to be criticizing Camus for not retaining the "cleansed" style of the opening lines of *L'Etranger*, he more or less admits that Meursault's duality, as reflected in Camus' style, is essential and artistically useful. So essential in fact, that along with novels by Flaubert,

Joyce, Kafka, and Faulkner, *L'Etranger* ranks as one of the generic sources of Robbe-Grillet's own work, particularly for *Le Voyeur*.

As in any derivative novel, there are similarities as well as differences. The most obvious resemblance between these two works is that a crime has taken place: Meursault has shot an Arab and Mathias has killed a thirteen-year-old girl. We know that in *L'Etranger* the sun has been accused of complicity in murder. Meursault tells us that "the day, already gorged with sun, slapped me in the face." In *Le Voyeur*, Robbe-Grillet uses an almost identical sequence to describe the objectification of Mathias' subconscious: "He sat down on the rock facing the sun," and "The tide was coming in"—"A small wave hit the rock with the sound of a slap." And a little later: "A bigger wave struck the sides of the rock with the sound of a slap." Mathias' attention focuses repeatedly on the increasing intensity of the "slapping" waves. These slaps and the way Mathias knocks on doors—he "hits" ("frapper" in French) between figure eight knot-holes—reveal a mounting inner tension and violence which will only be resolved with the sadistic murder of Jacqueline whom he presumably will slap and hit before she dies.

Throughout Camus' novel the sun is described as a "lumière aveuglante." This blinding light functions realistically enough but it is also a metaphysical symbol. The sun is its most dazzling the day of his mother's funeral and the day he shoots the Arab. And so, the "lover's quarrel" which Robbe-Grillet refers to in his article, seems to be Meursault's realization of man's contingency. This is his grudge against Nature, for swimming and lovemaking are part of man's honeymoon on earth (as Camus so beautifully describes it in his essay *Noces*). The sun's "slap" is a manifestation of Nature's indifference to joy and of the fact that all men must sooner or later die. Killing the Arab then is a metaphysical crime of passion. Meursault shoots the sun because he can not possess Nature for ever. Mathias' crime in *Le Voyeur* is also a crime of passion but it is not metaphysical in the same sense that Meursault's is. Mathias' crime is not a lover's quarrel, but the working out and resolution of a compulsive behavior pattern. Yet the result is the same. String, figure eights, knot-holes, blue cigarette wrappers, rusty piton, crabs legs, movie poster, etc., all act as cumulative stimuli which, like the sun and the sea in *L'Etranger*, precipitate his crime. It is brought to a climax slowly and gradually as a result of these multiple factors.

A similar cumulative effect of things, in Julien Green's novel *Le Voyageur sur la terre*, precipitates Daniel O'Donovan's death. His "madness" seems to stem from extreme fear—the fear that the steeple of a burning church which had once destroyed the house he is living in might, once again, as a result of a midnight fire, crush the house and kill him. But a sequential association completely represses the memory and significance of this event. O'Donovan, rather than face death, with all its metaphysical and philosophical implications of finality (is not this Meursault's problem?), goes insane. His madness seems to be a variant of Meursault's alienation:

> How could I have been mistaken so long and develop bonds to books, my money, myself, my tranquility? Was not real sadness the result of having felt victimized by everything I had wished for? I was so touched by this kind of revelation that I lay down on my bed so as not to fall over. The world could now end and life could go out of me. Everything visible existed only for my temptation and, in a shattering moment of decision, I rejected the possession of all these things, all earthly pretense, all hope of happiness on earth.[1]

The idea of death, coupled with an ephemeral happiness, seems to produce, in characters like Meursault and O'Donovan, states of dizziness and feelings of strangeness. These states may vary from a mild form of alienation to severe schizophrenia, as the Paul-Daniel O'Donovan split indicates. "Tragic complicity," as Robbe-Grillet defines it, may also lead to dizziness, alienation, sickness, and schizophrenia. The protagonists of his novels embody these characteristics in varying degrees.

Some critics have referred to inherent contradictions in the structure of *L'Etranger*. They have spoken of the anachronism between the shallow and unreflective Meursault of Part I and his extreme lucidity in Part II. This duality is, however, deliberate. In Part I Camus has purposely imitated Hemingway's style because it communicates most effectively the feeling of the "absurd." Death and solitude lead the Meursault of Part II towards analysis and reflection. It is in the second part of the novel that we become aware of the fact that he is not unintelligent. "The contradictions and anachronisms of his book are resolved," says Robbe-Grillet, "and the emotion to which we finally abandon ourselves without reserve is justified." [2] Meursault emerges, in spite of Part I, as a reasonably lucid protagonist. Mathias, on the other hand, does not achieve insight into his human condition and remains to the end a prisoner of the objects which precipitated his crime.

Meursault's four shots that fateful day on the beach are described as four sharp knocks on the door of misfortune. This detail also reveals a fundamental difference in motivation between Meursault and Mathias. Meursault, conscious that he has upset the natural balance of the world about him, does not conceal his crime. Mathias acts out his compulsive behavior and then conceals the evidence of his murder. Thus, Mathias' alienation differs fundamentally from Meursault's. Meursault is indifferent and a "stranger" only to the values of the organized society in which he lives. But he is in harmony with the "indifference" of the Universe. Mathias on the other hand, as Part II of *Le Voyeur* indicates, in which he tries to reconstruct a plausible alibi as well as to obliterate all evidence of his crime, cares enough about his place in society to want to remain alive. His concern is immediate and practical, he is not apprehended for the murder, he leaves the island, and the stylistic calm which pervades Part III of the novel, in contrast to the violence and tension of Part I, corresponds to a total absence of guilt. His earlier sense of guilt, manifest in the way he tries to fix a bicycle chain which needs no repair, reveals his orientation to society and the need for duplicity if he is to survive. Meursault, on the other hand, is incredibly honest, and it is in part this total honesty with himself and with others which is responsible for his undoing. He refuses to play the social game of mutual deception and though we may think him naïve he is at the same time admirable.

Meursault is not conscious of his great freedom until he is imprisoned, for then his absence of freedom is evidenced by the fact that he can no longer swim on the beach, or smoke, or make love. His absence of freedom leads him to substitute memory for real experience in the same way that Robbe-Grillet's protagonists, who are caught in the determinism of their compulsive drives, use memory and fantasy as an image always seen in the present:

> I would sometimes think about my room in my imagination.[3] I would start in one corner in order to return to it while enumerating mentally everything in my path. At first, it was a pretty fast job. But each time I began again, it took a little longer. I would remember each piece of furniture and in between any two pieces I would remember the place of every object and, for each object, all the details, and for the details themselves, an inlay, a crack, or a chipped edge, their color or grain. At the same time I would try not to lose the sequence of my inventory, to make a complete enumeration.

This detailed reconstruction of objects, like Borges' *Funes the Memorious* who, "lying on his back on his cot in the shadows, could imagine every crevice and every molding in the sharply defined houses surrounding him," [4] has, interestingly enough, become Robbe-Grillet's novelistic technique: whether Wallas in *Les Gommes* is looking at a tomato slice, or Mathias in *Le Voyeur* is watching the movement of waves over sea-weed, or the jealous husband in *La Jalousie* is reconstructing the stain of a centipede, or the protagonist of *Dans le labyrinthe* is watching the configurations of light reflected on a ceiling, or the unseen narrator in *L'Année dernière à Marienbad* is looking at the details of a baroque ceiling. These objectifications, these minute descriptions of objects which are an inherent part of Robbe-Grillet's novels are, for the reader, in the absence of inner monologue, one of two things: either the exteriorized image of the protagonist's psyche, or a demonstration of geometric "distance." Almost everything is seen in terms of an inner film of the mind's eye. And so, like Meursault in his cell, every one of Robbe-Grillet's protagonists (except X in *Marienbad*) is imprisoned within the determinism of a compulsive behavior pattern. Wallas in *Les Gommes* shoots his father because he has not resolved his Oedipus complex. Mathias is caught in the mesh of his psychosexual infantilism. The jealous husband's entire behavior pattern is limited to spying on his wife and, when she is away, to anxiety day-dreams. And the soldier of *Dans le labyrinthe* is a prisoner in the labyrinth and delirium of fever and exhaustion. A in *Marienbad* becomes a prisoner of the formal gardens. And so, as for Meursault in his cell, past and future are abolished. Only the present remains: "For me in my cell," says Meursault, "it was always the same day breaking like waves upon the shore and always the same goal I was pursuing."

Robbe-Grillet's protagonists blend reality with memory and fantasy in a continuous present incapable, as it were, of escaping the cell of their mind's eye. Robbe-Grillet has therefore adapted the allegorical meaning of *L'Etranger* in order to establish the absence of freedom of his own protagonists. Insomuch as Mathias is a prisoner of the objects and events which lead him to his crime, he is a victim of a "painful solidarity." The difference between the two, however, lies in the narrative. *L'Etranger* is narrated in the first person. Meursault is therefore free to humanize the world about him if he so desires or, more properly, depending on what Camus wishes to reveal about him at a particular time. *Le Voyeur* is apparently narrated in the third person, but this is deceptive, for the selection of detail—of reality, memory, or fantasy—is not done at random, nor does it, as in Balzac, correspond to a preconceived theory of the correspondences between the visible and invisible worlds, but depends on the mental set of the protagonist. And though Robbe-Grillet's article in the *NNRF* is an attack on the anthropomorphic metaphor, he has substituted a new narrative technique which appears to be different, but in reality is not. The waves which sound like slaps are an example of this device and the description is neither neutral nor "cleansed" as Robbe-Grillet would have us believe. For the subjectivity of Mathias is total and is then narrated as the inner film of his mind's eye which focuses selectively on one significant detail after another as he leads himself and the reader to the climax of sexual violence and murder. Robbe-Grillet apparently escapes from the anthropomorphic metaphor because of his remarkable handling of the objective correlative. This enables him as an author to remain detached while at the same time to describe Mathias' physical environment as well as his psyche.

Thus all of the environmental descriptions of Part I of *Le Voyeur* are catalysts to his crime. But they are also an objectification of how, presumably, a sex pervert is led to murder. And this is in part what Robbe-Grillet means when he says that his novels are "scientific." Descriptions of the waves for instance act as objective correlatives for Mathias' mounting sexual desire and thus become the objectification of his subconscious. A rusty piton, seaweed, and figure eight configurations become humanized in spite of Robbe-Grillet's "objective" technique. The whole discussion of "tragic Humanism" then becomes purely academic. Robbe-Grillet's novels have the virtue of being more difficult (if difficulty is a virtue) to penetrate, but, at the same time, they are also more absorbing. The reader must engage in the process of analysis which formerly the author performed for him. Thus, if Robbe-Grillet had written *L'Etranger* he would probably not have Meursault tell us about the photograph of the guillotine, for Meursault's imminent death would, we presume, lead him naturally to reflect on it and he might even imagine his own decapitation which, from the reader's point of view, would have fulfilled his last wish, namely that there be many spectators at his execution and that he be greeted with cries of hatred

Robbe-Grillet's *NNRF* article then seems to be nothing but a smoke screen, an attempt to enlighten his readers by indirection and a chance to poke some fun at the critics who, thoroughly misled by other similar articles, proceeded to negate all subjectivity and to focus their attention exclusively on the surface play of objects. But seemingly aware that the game is up, Robbe-Grillet recently described his novels as being entirely subjective. This means that his protagonists are still the victims of a "tragic Humanism." Is he not demonstrating the fallacy of humanizing the external world? For if we do humanize it, as do his protagonists, are we not negating our freedom, as did Meursault, and do we not then become, like Mathias, the prisoners of the very objects we have humanized?

ii

In the same *NNRF* article, "Nature, Humanisme, Tragédie," Robbe-Grillet criticizes Sartre for the manner in which Roquentin humanizes the world around him. Once more, however, the question is academic. Roquentin, in his search for meaning, freedom, and identity escapes from the prison walls (figuratively speaking of course) which had determined his life, and moves slowly, but nevertheless progressively towards the realization that a creative act is perhaps the manifestation of man's greatest freedom; that the man who wrote and the negress who sings "Some of these days/you'll miss me honey" are, if only temporarily, escaping from the contingency of their existence.

None of Robbe-Grillet's personages (except X in *Marienbad*) achieve such insight. This is not meant to be a critique of his method, merely a statement of fact. Robbe-Grillet might even be making a more forceful statement about man's freedom by writing novels demonstrating its absence. As everyone knows, freedom for Sartre depends on choice. Man's successive choices determine what he is and what he will be and man is free to the extent that he deliberately chooses to affirm himself through action. Sartre brings Roquentin to the threshold of action and there the novel ends. Robbe-Grillet's two novels (*Les Gommes* and *Dans le labyrinthe*), which represent a quest not unlike Roquentin's, reveal no such insight on the protagonist's part. But here we have a curious paradox. True to his formula of author effacement and reader participation, Robbe-Grillet's characters do not achieve insight but pave the way for reader illumination. Wallas' search for an alleged murderer is a disguise for the deeper meaning of the novel, for, had he been able to resolve his Oedipus complex, he would not have shot his father.[5]

On one level the novel must be read as his search for this inner truth which he vaguely apprehends but cannot grasp and, on another level, his failure is an inevitable concomitant of the necessity to enlighten the reader. Thus Wallas is the unwitting victim of his own Oedipus complex and the detective, ironically, turns out to be the murderer in question. The tired, fever-wracked soldier in *Dans le labyrinthe* dies in his attempt to deliver the insignificant contents of a shoe-box to a man whose name he cannot remember and whom he is supposed to meet on a street whose name he has forgotten in a city in which he is a stranger. One cannot say that the reader's imagination is in error if he should establish an analogy between this novel, *L'Etranger*, *The Castle*, and *Waiting for Godot* and, if in doing so, he comes to some conclusion about man's fate and his relation to God and the Universe. The soldier-messenger dies in his ignorance but hopefully the reader will not, and to the extent that the reader is capable of unravelling the labyrinthine paradox he develops insight into the meaning of existence. Thus the job of elucidation which Roquentin performs for the reader (as a spokesman for Sartre) must be performed in Robbe-Grillet's novels by the reader himself.

Though Robbe-Grillet's technique as a novelist differs from Sartre's it is, nevertheless, strongly dependent on his thought as philosopher and theoretician. Robbe-Grillet admits that he was never able to finish or understand *L'Etre et le néant* (*Being and Nothingness*), yet his novels, by stressing the distance between man and things, suggest the void, the "nothingness," which is the basis for so much of Sartre's theoretical writing. Nevertheless, it is this very distance which Roquentin tries to abolish. The purely visual geometric description which limits itself to measuring, situating, and defining an object in space is Robbe-Grillet's method when a protagonist is calm and remains detached from his environment: "In addition, instead of being rectangular like the one [banana grove] above it, this plot has the form of a trapezium; since the edge which constitutes the inferior line is not perpendicular to its two sides—lower and upper—in themselves parallel. The right side (that is the lower) has only thirteen banana trees left, instead of twenty-three." (*La Jalousie*, p. 34.) Roquentin eschews comparable geometric descriptions in favor of anthropomorphic ones. Not unlike Meursault, he refers to the "true" sea that "grovels" beneath a thin green film. The "cold" light of the sun is a "strict judgment." He notes the "happy death-rattle" of a fountain or the leather-covered seat of a trolley-car which becomes a "dead ass," or the Autodidact's hand which is a "fat white worm." The most highly charged emotional object for Roquentin is, of course, the chestnut-tree root. Its metamorphoses run from a "black fingernail," to "boiled leather," to "mildew," to a "dead snake," to a "vulture's claw," an "obese foot," a "seal skin," and so on.

Robbe-Grillet's own personages, whenever they become personally involved with their environment, behave in ways analogous to those of Meursault and Roquentin. The cool and calculated detachment which a geometric description communicates between the husband (in *La Jalousie*) and his banana plantation is there in order to demonstrate a metaphysical distance—the inevitable distance between animate and inanimate things. Mathias, as long as he is counting watches and evaluating possible profits, manifests a similar detachment which disappears, however, under the impact of his compulsion. The husband's relationship to his wife, to Franck, to the centipede, or to any object which is an analogue for his jealousy

is the opposite of detachment. He is, for instance, highly
critical of the way Franck eats his soup wheras A... for
him is the epitome of daintiness and good manners.
Franck's hands are described in terms which remind us
of the Autodidact's hand in *La Nausée*. The descriptions
of A... combing her hair are remarkable for the quality
of their sensuous detail. The *stain* of the centipede on
the wall is, of course, the most vivid objective correlative
of his jealousy. This stain contaminates all other stains,
with the result that few objects remain "cleansed" or
"neutral." The husband's attention or memory returns
repeatedly to a gravy mark Franck's knife has made on
the white table cloth. An oil stain on the road demands
his attention. A lamp casts a "stain" of light on the surrounding darkness. A larger bug flying around the lamp
will be seen as a spot ("la tache vient s'y heurter avec violence"). Moisture spots as well as shadows are associated
with stains in a continuous and progressive obsession
which at last forces the husband to erase the mark of the
centipede on the wall in a desperate attempt to rid himself
of the agonizing pangs of fear and jealousy.

Stain and shadow are also related to color. Whenever
some object or action triggers the husband's jealousy,
neutral descriptions of the banana plantation, which the
husband-reader sees in terms of line and plane, metamorphose into descriptions using color and texture. Color,
unlike form, tends to change with the lighting, the back-
ground, and the perceiver. We are not surprised, therefore,
since color is so much more personal than geometry, to
find that Roquentin's eyes are drawn, not to lines and
contour, but to the uncertain shades of color which hide
the object. If it is not touch it is usually the sight of an
uncertain color that upsets him and causes his "nausea."
("Colors, tastes, odors were never true, never really themselves and nothing but themselves." [6]) Color, concludes
Robbe-Grillet, has the same effect on the eyes as physical
contact on the palm of one's hand. The extent to which
Robbe-Grillet's personages react to their environment in
terms of pure geometric form or in terms of color, meta-

phor, or anthropomorphic adjective, reveals the extent to which they remain detached from or become involved with the objects as projections of their inner selves. The moment involvement begins the husband will not refer to the triangle or the parallelepiped of the banana grove but to its "green mass," or to "the reddish earth," and then, later, to the blue stationery on which A... is writing to Franck, or to the texture of the grain of the wood on the banister under the peeling paint (not unrelated to stains) and progressively to the more "intimate" color of Franck's white shirt or of A...'s black hair.

There are virtually no tactile or olfactory sensations in Robbe-Grillet's novels. Perception is primarily visual, less frequently auditory. This is due to the fact that sight not only includes many degrees of perception, but is, according to Robbe-Grillet, the most efficient way of recording the separation between man and objects. An optical description, he says, is the best device with which to record the inherent neutrality of things since the human glance, devoid of tactile sensations, or uncontaminated by color, allows them to remain in their respective places. Whenever Robbe-Grillet's protagonists "contaminate" objects or the landscape it is because and whenever the author wishes to communicate obliquely to the reader the effect of a deep-seated emotion on the behavior of a particular personage. Beneath the Selective Omniscience of the jealous husband's perceptions lies the Editorial Omniscience of Robbe-Grillet's judgment which is manifest, not by his obtrusive interference in the narrative, as with Hardy, but in the distinction between the geometric form of objects (their neutrality or inability to influence human behavior) and their color and texture which in Robbe-Grillet's novels are the expression of an evolving "complicity." The slightest mention or thought of A... eliminates geometry and immediately introduces color and texture. An oil lamp with bugs flying around it is at first described with the scientific objectivity of electrons revolving around the nucleus of an atom: "They are only simple particles in movement, which describe more or less flattened ellipses along horizontal planes, or very feeble tilts, which cross the elongated gas-mantle at varying levels" (*La Jalousie*, p. 148). One of the bugs which falls on the table-top and which begins to crawl, bears some resemblance to a centipede. This resemblance is enough to contaminate all "neutrality" and from that moment on the silence of the night is full of density and sounds replete with anxiety and portent due to A...'s failure to return as planned after her trip into town with Franck. Henceforth the husband will know little peace of mind as he imagines A... and Franck in bed, A... and Franck crashing into a tree, A... asleep etc.

The reader, through the protagonist, is therefore subject to interesting gradations in perception. A purely geometric description of things means that a personage is calmly detached, capable of accepting the distance between himself and the world. The geometry, however, is Robbe-Grillet's attempt to force the reader into a similar detachment. Things which are described geometrically, "relate only to themselves, with no chinks or crevices for us to slip into, and without causing us the least dizziness," says Robbe-Grillet in his essay on "Nature, Humanisme, Tragédie." If Roquentin and the jealous husband cannot maintain this detachment it is first and obviously because their respective authors did not wish them to (hence Robbe-Grillet's critique of *La Nausée* which is again academic and which draws attention to his own technique by indirection), and secondly, in making them the victims of "tragic complicity" they are both working out artistic theories of the "absurd."

In Robbe-Grillet's novels the essence of Sartre's existential theory has been assimilated into an indistinguishable blend of form and content whereas Roquentin, in *La Nausée*, is clearly Sartre's spokesman. We conclude from what Roquentin says and from his multifarious reactions to things, particularly to the black root of the tree, that existence is characterized by the presence of interior distances, and that "nausea" is the painful visceral penchant felt by man for these distances. But Robbe-Grillet, in his analysis of *La Nausée*, stops short of the main point of the novel, namely that if "nausea" is the painful visceral penchant for these distances, it is, nevertheless, a temporary phenomenon, a by-product of the bringing to consciousness of this realization which, after all, is what *La Nausée* is about. The fact that Roquentin anthropomorphizes his environment is perfectly consistent with the purpose of the novel. Sartre, on the first page has Roquentin deliberately discard a visual geometric world in favor of the charged visceral content of color (see, for instance, the long description of the shifting colors of the suspenders), texture, anthropomorphic adjective, and metaphor. On the first page of *La Nausée* Roquentin says, apropos a cardboard ink-bottle container: "It's a rectangular parallelepiped, it stands out against—this is idiotic, there is nothing to say about it. One must avoid such things and not look for something strange where there is nothing." Roquentin then proceeds to record everything impressionistically. Yet "not to look for something strange where there is nothing," would be a tacit recognition of the "distance" Robbe-Grillet is talking about. *This "distance" is the philosophical basis of his novels.*

Hardy is his own spokesman through Editorial intrusion. Sartre's spokesman is Roquentin. Robbe-Grillet's judgment is "built into" his novel. Since authorial intrusion blocks the intimate nature of the artistic experience he has had to devise a technique which will do "double duty"—a technique which will tell the story and at the same time contain a judgment of that story. Art is a language and every artist finally evolves his own hieroglyph. Robbe-Grillet's theoretical writings help to explain his art but they by no means communicate the experience of it. Mathias, for instance, is the victim of "tragic complicity." The novel demonstrates how he is led to murder, how an inherently "neutral" object like a blue cigarette wrapper floating on the water can, when combined with other objects which are anthropomorphized, reveal the nature of Mathias' unconscious selectivity and at the same time represent for the reader (in the absence of inner monologue) an initial image of sexuality and violence. Such objective correlatives—that is, the visible image of an inner state of mind—(like the centipede) are the hard core of the outside world which surrounds a protagonist, but the fact that the centipede comes to stand for the husband's jealousy reveals how the novelist can project the inner state of mind of a character into what appears to be simply a description of landscape. This device enables the novelist to describe, simultaneously, the "unseen" subconscious mind of a character, his physical environment, and the extent to which he is anthropomorphizing his environment. It is the "neutrality" or the "complicity" of the description which communicates the judgment of the author on his character. The novel will then depend on the total and final interrelationship of these three factors: symbol, geometric distance, and complicity.

Robbe-Grillet's method blends the subjectivity of a personage whose eye, unlike a random photograph, selects specific details from his environment, with the purely objective description necessitated to communicate the impersonality of a neutral Universe. He has thus tried, and in my opinion, achieved a literary tour-de-force—that of fusing the subjective point of view of a character with his own "objective" interpretation of the world. Robbe-Grillet can thus communicate the subjective point of view of a man in the throes of jealousy with the rational controlled observation of the novelist whose intervention is not readily discernible. This is perhaps the element which puzzles and bores so many readers. The description and enumeration of trees in a banana grove serve to give us a contrast to and some measure of relief from the mania of the husband's jealousy but also, no doubt, to provide, in addition to the author's calculated objectivity and with an absolute economy of means some information about the protagonist's occupation. This simultaneity of two points of view depends on narrative style—the careful selection of objective correlatives—which, for the *reader*, will represent the protagonist's inner world and yet, for the protagonist, are the objective reality of the outside world. It is this factor which has enabled Robbe-Grillet to write novels of objective "subjectivity."

Robbe-Grillet, in one of the strongest anti-Bergsonian statements ever made, contends that only science is capable of describing the interior essence of things. Objects in themselves will therefore forever remain neutral, not because science is neutral but because objects are inanimate. The novelist's function will be, in part, to communicate this neutrality, which Hardy's Tess so obviously violates, while at the same time showing that a character who breaches this "distance" between himself and the world (which is what *his* novels so far have been about) is acting as though these neutral objects were not separate from but projections of himself. Hardy's Editorial Omniscience intervenes to enlighten the reader while in Robbe-Grillet's novels the contrast between objects described geometrically and objects which have been contaminated by a character's inner passion, desire, or derangement serve in lieu of Editorial Omniscience. The reader must, if he is to understand the philosophical intent of the novel, distinguish between the *nature* of objects described in these *two* ways and the purpose of a novelist who makes the reader see the world through the eyes of a protagonist. But Robbe-Grillet hopes, no doubt, that the reader will be conscious of this distinction whereas the protagonist obviously is not. There is no authorial intrusion in the Hardy sense but judgment is not lacking. It is now a function of form rather than the result of direct intervention.

Critics have consistently misinterpreted Robbe-Grillet's theoretical writings and his novelistic technique which, as everyone knows, consists of minute and detailed visual descriptions of objects and things, virtually *ad nauseam*. What they have failed to distinguish and differentiate was the simultaneity of the two points of view: the protagonist's and the author's. Virtually everything that is described in his novels, though the descriptions themselves reveal the difference, is seen through the eyes of one of the personages. It would seem that in *La Jalousie* the entire point of view sequence is that of the jealous husband who spies on his wife through the jalousies and who registers with infinite variation the contour of a centipede on the wall or the geometric shapes of banana groves. While the selectivity stems from the choice of the jealous protagonist the descriptions themselves are, of course, Robbe-Grillet's. We now have an effective blend of Selective and Editorial Omniscience. No observer consciously registers objects with the precise, detached and geometric objectivity which has, by now, become the trademark of Robbe-Grillet's technique. Geometric figures, however, are the pure outlines of substance, and in themselves they describe the perfect nature of a rational universe. Thus matter occupies space and assumes forms. Since, according to Robbe-Grillet, man cannot know the inside of things, the world around him reverts to a smooth surface without meaning, without soul, and without values. To communicate this the novelist must construct its surface and its independence. Such descriptions will refuse any idea of pre-established order. The fact that objects in *Le Voyeur* act as catalysts for Mathias and precipitate his crime is the illustration of tragic complicity between man and the world. There exists a pre-established order for Mathias even though it may be absent from the Universe. The "order" stems from all those predisposing homicidal tendencies residing within him. His own passionate involvement with stimuli of the outside world—bits of string, rusty pitons, cigarette wrappers, sea-gulls, etc.—breaks down the neutrality of the world, appropriates it and subsequently makes him the victim of his exteriorized desire. A similar process governs Wallas' activities in *Les Gommes*.

Robbe-Grillet's novelistic technique then combines the unique *simultaneity* of two points of view: the Selective Omniscience of the jealous husband who sees what he must because of his uncontrollable passion and the hidden Editorial Omniscience of the author who describes objects as though they were being registered "objectively" on film. Mathias' passion is exteriorized by virtue of the selectivity of his roving eye, but what he sees is described the way Robbe-Grillet wants the reader to see. This explains the interminable description of the banana grove in *La Jalousie* whose function it is, not only to give us information on the husband's work, but also to render an objective Cartesian distance between him (us) and the world around him (us). The novel is a tour de force for not only has the novelist been refined out of existence (an illusion of course), but so also has the protagonist. The jealous husband who is never once described, or seen, registers the behavior and activity of his wife A... and her presumed lover Franck. The reader gradually realizes that he, the reader, must identify completely with the point of view of the jealous husband and if we, the readers, follow the evolution of this jealousy to its climax we gain insight into the torment and pangs of jealousy which have been exteriorized (as they would be in a movie) and which do not rely on any kind of interior monologue. Hence the obsessive and oneiric quality of Robbe-Grillet's descriptions. This novel would seem to be the final and logical conclusion of the novelist's preoccupation with point of view. The novelist *appears* to have eliminated himself and instead of judging his characters overtly he makes the reader formulate the author's judgment for himself.

One senses here, in relation to the whole question of point of view and Robbe-Grillet's attempt to determine perception and memory as structures, the influence of Hüsserlian phenomenology. Robbe-Grillet has tried to capture the pure interior essence of self, not in the Platonic sense of an Ideal essence, but in terms of the relationship between consciousness and the perception of things. It is this rapport, this "eidetic reduction," as Hüsserl calls it, which forms the basis of Robbe-Grillet's art.

The descriptions of a Selective Omniscience are not mere photographs. The selectivity of his protagonists is a reflection of their psychic needs and preoccupations. This is not the world of Christopher Isherwood's *I am a Camera*, recording at random scenes in Berlin but, in the case of Mathias, the deterministic world of a sex maniac caught in the web of his own murderous complicity. These offspring of Robbe-Grillet's imagination then resemble Racine's heroines who are also bound by the rigorous determinism of their loves and hates. Robbe-Grillet's heroes are not free. They are as much the victims of their passions as are Racine's heroines. This also explains why dialogue is so infrequent in Robbe-Grillet's novels for his characters are the isolated marionettes of Baudelaire's "hypocrite lecteur." They are in a world of "no exit," the slaves of their desires or of their external stimuli which lead them to anthropomorphize a neutral or indifferent world.

If man cries out and no one answers, says Robbe-Grillet, then indeed there is no one to hear the cry. The protagonists of Malraux, Sartre, and Camus, however, act as though someone were there but refuses to answer. These "existential" writers enhance this "absence" or this "solitude" with a depth of meaning, content, and even soul. This distance between man who calls and presumably God who does not answer engenders anguish and this anguish, they say, is in turn capable of giving meaning to life. It is from this premise that the concepts of man's "dreadful freedom," and "l'homme délaissé," have evolved. Camus' use of the Sisyphus myth, *Caligula*'s logical madness, and the fraternal bond of *Man's Fate* are further elaborations of "existential" tragedy. "Existential" thinkers from Pascal through Kierkegaard to present-day existentialism have suffered and trembled. "The silence of these infinite spaces scares me," said Pascal. The silence Pascal refers to is, we infer, the absence of an answer to his call.

Can man escape tragedy, asks Robbe-Grillet? "I claim," he says, "that man, some day, will free himself of it. But I have no proof of the future. For me also, it is a *bet*. 'Man is a sick animal,' wrote Unamuno in *The Tragic Sense of Life*. The bet is in believing that he can be cured, and that if this is true it would be folly to shut him up forever in his present sickness and unhappiness. I have nothing to lose. The bet, all things considered, is the only reasonable one." [7]

Whither lies the cure? I suspect, if the bondage of Robbe-Grillet's present hero is any indication, that it lies in the direction of the freedom of the Cornelian hero who, like Augustus in his clemency (pardons those who plotted to assassinate him instead of punishing them), is able to say "I am master of myself as I am master of the Universe." It is this freedom which transforms Corneille's heroes into such modern protagonists. Robbe-Grillet's heroes are the victims and not the masters of the world they inhabit. His novels to date indicate that man is subservient to his own sense of tragic complicity. Insomuch as man does not seem to have evolved beyond this stage Robbe-Grillet's novels are a reflection of and a statement on the human condition. Might we expect his subsequent works to move in the direction of freedom so dear to Sartre?—and to Corneille?

A NOVEL
     OF OBJECTIVE SUBJECTIVITY:
     THE VOYEUR

DURING AN INTERVIEW with Jacques Brenner, published
in *Arts* (March 1953), Robbe-Grillet asserted that *Les
Gommes* is a descriptive and scientific novel. In January
1959, in an interview with Denise Bourdet, Robbe-Grillet
stated that "scientific observation consists in describing
without interpreting, in never giving meaning to things." [1]
His novels are noteworthy indeed for their absence of
analysis, and readers familiar with his descriptive method
will have no difficulty concluding that if *Les Gommes*
is a "scientific novel," so also are *Le Voyeur*, *La Jalousie*,
and *Dans le labyrinthe*. But in what way are these novels
"scientific?" Is Robbe-Grillet initiating a "new realism"
as has been suggested, or is it more accurately a new
naturalism? If we may be permitted to define naturalism
as a realism with scientific pretensions, and if we apply
the rigorous pattern of Freudian determinism—provided
we accept Freud's method as "scientific"—to the psychic
and mental operations of Mathias in *Le Voyeur*, and of
the jealous husband in *La Jalousie*, then these novels
would seem to qualify as naturalistic.

Far from Zola's dubious hereditary theories, Robbe-
Grillet's naturalism stems from his attempt to create a
psychoanalytic case-study in fictional form. Indeed,
Robbe-Grillet himself has hinted that a psychoanalytic
interpretation of Mathias' behavior might give fruitful

results.[2] Yet Roland Barthes, who has focused his attention on the purely external relationships of objects, considers any mention of Mathias' pathology irrelevant.[3] Champigny declares that Mathias is a psychoanalytic case, but that *Le Voyeur* is not a psychoanalytic novel, and on these grounds he refuses to analyze the character of Mathias.[4] This conclusion seems to me bizarre. Moreover, when Champigny suggests that "the monstrous part of Mathias remains in its original darkness," [5] he fails to perceive that Mathias' psychic evolution has been skilfully objectified into consistent images (even the murder of the thirteen-year-old Jacqueline is announced in this way). Nothing remains dark if we accept and apply Freud's theory of free association to Mathias' sadism, his daydreaming, his memory flashbacks, and his distortion of reality (the shifts in chronology and the dislocation of time-space in *Le Voyeur* has an inner necessity lacking in *Les Gommes*). All this is perhaps best understood in terms of some kind of "inner film." Such images of the mind are what Robbe-Grillet calls "des imaginations," and though they function in the present, they may involve distant landscapes, future meetings with people, or the details of a past encounter. At other times, says Robbe-Grillet, connection with the immediate reality of the external world is maintained, in contrast to the inner film of the mind's eye. "Thus the total film of our mind accepts simultaneously, in turn, and with equal intensity fragments of reality suggested by sight or sound, with fragments of a past, distant, future or totally fantastic reality." [6]

The dislocation of time can perhaps be clarified if we compare *Le Voyeur* to Julien Green's *Le Voyageur sur la terre*. Both O'Donovan and the thirteen-year-old Jacqueline die under mysterious circumstances and the townspeople, in both cases, advance various hypotheses to explain the "accident." Robbe-Grillet has actually used a travelling salesman for his murder while the "murderer" in Green's case, though real enough for O'Donovan (and also for the reader), turns out to be the vision of a hallucination. O'Donovan's thrice recurrent dream which anticipates his death is clearly a dream even though the description itself is that of an eventual reality. The delineation between dream and reality for Robbe-Grillet's characters (and hence for his readers) is not clear and so the immediacy of a future event, which may only be a dream or an imagination, gives it the substance of the reality it may eventually become. Of course Green's first person narrative has been transformed by Robbe-Grillet into an objective third person description of the protagonist's psyche as a function of his environment. Green anticipates this in various ways in his own novels but Robbe-Grillet has carried it to its ultimate and logical conclusion.

Le Voyeur is not a novel of allegorical fantasy like *Don Quixote*. *Don Quixote* is by no means a "scientific novel in the sense in which we mean it here. Robbe-Grillet has purposely devised a kind of case-study in which Mathias' "temps mental" recreates the dimensions of his inner time-space (since the dislocations will be those of his mind in response to his psychic dictates and needs), which will depend on memory, daydreams, and his perception of reality, all mixed, blended, and juxtaposed, with no attention to chronology—clock chronology—since Mathias' psychic chronology follows its own laws. The absence of analysis by both author and protagonist is significant, because it is those novels from which analysis and coherent introspection are absent that are psychologically the most interesting. The reader, then, becomes the "analyst": he must solve the behavior of the protagonist instead of having it explained for him; he must perceive and establish the function of the relationships hidden beneath the visible surface "play" of objects. Like Maupassant, Robbe-Grillet is, in this sense, an "objective novelist." Their technique is in fact so similar that Maupassant's statement from his introduction to *Pierre et Jean* may also be applied to Robbe-Grillet: "The psychology in the book must be hidden as it is hidden in reality within the acts of existence." Instead of explaining or describing the state of mind of his character, the objective novelist presents the action or gesture which, in a particular situation, the character's state of mind leads him fatally to perform. We shall see shortly how this method works in Mathias' case. Moreover, it is not a contradiction to assert that this extreme "objectivity" is "subjective." Robbe-Grillet insists that

> the subjectivity is even greater than it is in the traditional novel, in which the narrator seems, more frequently than not, outside the story he is telling, outside of the world itself, a kind of demiurge. This subjectivity is I believe— and contrary to what is usually thought—the essential trait of what has been called "the new novel." It is precisely this which Nathalie Sarraute's work and mine have in common and which critics have often sought to oppose. The whole contemporary novel since the beginning of the century has tended in this direction.[7]

Nathalie Sarraute has made this same point in *L'Ere du soupçon* (Paris, 1956). The "new" novelist, and Robbe-Grillet in particular, in his attempt to be "scientific" and to involve the reader in a way in which the most traditional novels do not, has abandoned the "analyse psychologique" of, for example, the *Princesse de Clèves* and *Adolphe*, in favor of a method more characteristic of Faulkner or Kafka (two of Robbe-Grillet's most influential precursors).[8] Using a cinematographic technique of minute and detailed visualization, Robbe-Grillet sees the new novel as a "devinette" to be deciphered (*Les Gommes*), or as a puzzle whose image has to be situated in terms of time-space (*Le Voyeur, La Jalousie*), or as a detective game,[9] to which the reader brings all his knowledge and alertness in order to reconstruct the plot. He also frequently sees various parts of the novel in terms of a picture or pictures; in terms of an immense objective correlative which, once understood, becomes the key to one or more aspects of the novel. A picture of Thebes in *Les Gommes* gives us the Greek motif and is one of the main clues to an Oedipal interpretation of the novel. The movie posters in *Le Voyeur* are the objectification of Mathias' three different states of mind. The picture of boats on a calendar in *La Jalousie*, to which the husband's eye returns obsessively at intervals, corresponds to his morbid fear that his wife will leave him. In *Dans le labyrinthe*, the picture of the "Defeat of Reichenfels" is the motif for the entire novel.

But more important still, the new novel, specifically that of Robbe-Grillet, though obviously Nathalie Sarraute, Michel Butor, Claude Simon, and others also qualify, is much like modern nonobjective painting. Nathalie Sarraute, again in *L'Ere du soupçon*, has pointed out this resemblance. The shifts in chronology and time-space, the usual absence of plot (which, however, can be reconstructed in *Le Voyeur*), the absence of strong characterization, and of names (the jealous husband has no name in *La Jalousie*, and his wife is identified only by the letter A)—all are indicative of the revolt of the new writers against the traditional novel. But this revolt is not all negative, nor has it "dehumanized" the novel and the characters as Roland Barthes[10] and Colette Audry[11] maintain. It has merely shifted the level of humanization. As Robbe-Grillet observes: "The contemporary novel, which has been accused of wishing to exclude man from the universe, gives him, in reality, the role of observer and puts him in the front seat."[12] Thus, in *Le Voyeur*, he must become a psychoanalytic sleuth if he is to grasp the inner necessity and artistry of that novel. Wallas' sleuthing in *Les Gommes* gives us a clue as to how Robbe-Grillet's novels are to be read. The eraser marked "di," with "Oe——pe" missing, is a case in point. The window decoration with the Greek motif is, as Morrissette has pointed out,[13] the objective correlative of Wallas' Oedipus complex. But the correlation in this first novel is not convincing and not dynamic; it lacks the inner necessity of *Le Voyeur* in which Mathias' perceptions focus obsessively on a violent sexual decor.

The detective in *Les Gommes* is performing the task which the reader himself must perform in *Le Voyeur*. If the reader is to solve Mathias' crime, he must determine the meaning of the pictured objective correlatives. Wallas, the detective in *Les Gommes* who is searching for the murderer, shoots his own father, and because he has failed to solve the meaning of the Oedipal sequences presented to him, he turns out to be the murderer in question. In *La Jalousie*, the reader, if he is to understand the novel, must "see" with the eyes of the jealous husband. But to "see" what the husband sees, the reader must piece together the evidence as a detective might assemble clues in order to form the picture of total insight.

In the case of *Le Voyeur*, the reader must reconstruct the events and their chronology, if he is to understand first, that a crime has taken place (which many critics have failed to grasp), and second, how it took place, psychologically and artistically, though to separate the two is arbitrary and useful only for the sake of discussion. ("Art has always been *form* and I would willingly assert that in my eyes the content of a work of art is precisely its form.")[14]

One of the most effective devices with which to involve the reader, as such modern novelists as Hemingway and Faulkner have demonstrated, is the substitution of Selective and Multiple Omniscience for Editorial Omniscience. Robbe-Grillet has objectified the states of mind of his protagonist (particularly in *Le Voyeur* and *La Jalousie*) as images of a Selective Omniscience. Since these images depend on a description of objects, Roland Barthes has suggested that "the object is, in this case, no longer a vehicle of affinities, a proliferation of sensations and symbols: it offers only an optical resistance."[15] But objects rarely exist independently of Mathias' perception. They do not appear, in this novel, gratuitously, as Roland Barthes maintains.[16] They are contingent on Mathias' state of mind. In an article in *Le Monde*, Robbe-Grillet himself insists that readers and critics have exaggerated the isolated importance of objects: "One should notice also, it seems to me, that these descriptions are always made by *somebody*. Nothing is shown of the material world than what a personage sees or, if need be, imagines."[17] But Robbe-Grillet is not entirely honest when he claims that the entire novel reflects Mathias' point of view. This is true if we limit our insight to the realistic level. If we go beyond the mere description of objects, we see that the objective correlatives are manipulated with great skill, and in such a way as to envelop Mathias in a deterministic pattern of things and events from which he cannot extricate himself.

Robbe-Grillet is such a clever craftsman that these objective stimuli and Mathias' point of view blend imperceptibly into one artistic pattern. "Tout en bas de la paroi verticale sans *garde-fou* [my italics], son regard plongea vers l'eau, qui montait et descendait contre la pierre. L'ombre de la *jetée* [my italics] la colorait d'un vert sombre, presque noir." [18] The double meaning of "garde-fou" (railing but also a play on the word "mad" or "madness") and "la jetée (jetty but also a play on the word "thrown") add weight to the artistry of the deterministic web woven around Mathias. He *is* "mad" and Jacqueline will be "thrown" from the cliff into the water after she has been murdered.

Robbe-Grillet's precursor here is, of course, Flaubert. The web of determinism which he weaves around Emma Bovary is beautiful and deadly to behold. Emma finds herself trapped by a banal and vulgar existence which is an absolute contrast to her imaginary world of romantic bliss. Her dilemma stems from the impossibility of reconciling desire and fulfillment; and the progression of events within the novel all contribute to justify and explain her final desperate suicidal act which, in a curious and anachronistic way, is her one and only act of freedom.

Mathias, in Le Voyeur, is also enmeshed in the determinism of events and the material world around him which leads to the murder of the thirteen-year-old girl Jacqueline. In this sense both works are cause-and-effect novels. In each one we are presented, not with an analysis of what prompts suicide or murder, but with a series of encounters, reactions, actions, and involvements which lead the reader to conclude and to accept, without the slightest doubt, that Emma's suicide and Mathias' murder, as acts, are logical and inevitable consequences of a certain behavior pattern.

The talented novelist will use the environment of his characters, not as a neutral decor in which to situate them (and for which any decor would do), but as the only and inevitable material environment which will correspond to the workings of their deranged psyches. Thus, in a Freudian sense, the warped personality of a fictional hero can give the reader insight into the workings of a normal mind. The novelist can lead his protagonist from one situation or event to another using the environment as a function of character; what the reader sees and reads about depends upon the inner necessity of the protagonists' biased perceptions. The abnormal world becomes plausible because of the undeniable materiality of the fictional world which surrounds the character.

We must be careful, however, to make two distinctions and to determine, *à propos* of any "objective" novel such as *Madame Bovary*, *Une Vie*, or *Le Voyeur*, whether the objective correlatives are the function of an Editorial Omniscience or whether, as with *Le Voyeur*, they are a blend of Editorial and Selective Omniscience. The answer to this question will reveal precisely how Robbe-Grillet's novels differ from those of his "objective" precursors: Flaubert and Maupassant.

In *La Jalousie* Robbe-Grillet has effaced himself completely in order to give absolute play to the subjective jealousy of the husband who spies on the activities of his wife through the "jalousies" of the windows. The ambivalence of the word "jalousie" corresponds to the inner world of the husband's emotions as well as to the external world of people, objects, and events which feed this jealousy. The nature of the husband's perceptions will depend upon the intensity of his emotional state. The centipede in this sense is much more than an animal on the wall. On the narrative level it helps to define the surroundings of a banana plantation: the fact that such animals lurk in dark corners of houses and are sometimes seen in the light of day or of lamps; the way in which A... grasps the table cloth with her fingers while Franck is crushing the centipede (it is the jealous husband who is looking at his wife's hand) reveals either a horror of the centipede or anxiety for Franck (which?). It is the obsessive quality of these images that will haunt the husband's memory and imagination and which, in turn, leads the reader to conclude that the centipede and the stain on the wall are the exteriorized image of the husband's jealousy. This tension and ambivalence of the protagonist's inner and outer world constitutes the poetry of such novels. In the world in which Mathias or the jealous husband move, every incident, no matter how insignificant, will relate to and shed light on the meaning and elaboration of an obsession. The centepede which crawls out of a hiding place in order to pause in plain view half-way up the dining room wall, is an analogue to the husband's jealousy which lurks in the dark recesses of his subconscious. Jealousy has, at last, been rendered visible—rendered visible by the Selective Omniscience of the husband. The Editorial Omniscience of the "invisible" author transforms the centipede into an objective correlative. Robbe-Grillet's objective correlatives most frequently, though not always, are seen by the protagonist but interpreted by the reader.

The movement of the sea in *Le Voyeur*, in analogous fashion, becomes the objective correlative for the workings of Mathias' subconscious. If the blue cigarette wrapper floating on the surface represents Mathias' haunting obsession with a scene of impending violence witnessed earlier that day, then the way in which the piece of blue paper submerges and emerges with the to-and-fro motion of the water (this "breathing" of the ocean reveals "langorous" strands of sea-weed and the sound of the waves is like a "slap"), then this description is the writer's only way (short of actual analysis and explanation which Robbe-Grillet refuses to use) of describing what is going on in Mathias' mind, since he himself is not aware of this subconscious activity and therefore could not give us an inner monologue.

We cannot separate form and content in these novels nor even speak about plot without describing it in terms of visible technique. Everything Mathias sees and does is either a catalyst for his crime or an objective correlative for his subconscious. Nothing is extraneous. These works employ an economy of means worthy of the finest French classical tragedies. On this level the reader will always be aware of the author's artistic presence. The author of such works of art is, as Flaubert would have him, like God, present everywhere and visible nowhere. But unlike Emma Bovary's environment, which is frequently described in terms of an Editorial Omniscience in order to enlighten the reader or to convey information, Mathias' or the jealous husband's environment is almost entirely subordinate to and a function of their Selective Omniscience. In *Le Voyeur* and in *La Jalousie* the point of view depends on what Mathias or the jealous husband see. In *Madame Bovary* the point of view is constantly shifting from Editorial to Multiple Omniscience.

The novel begins with the author's narrative, shifts to Charles, or to Emma or to Léon but, in the final analysis is subordinate to Flaubert's total vision. This subordination to a total vision is of course true of any novelist. But it is always a question of degree. Faulkner's Multiple Omniscience in *The Sound and the Fury* is obviously a variant of Balzac's Editorial Omniscience. But since the modern author as God is "suspect," Multiple or Selective Omniscience give the reader a greater illusion of "truth" than does the Editorial Omniscience. Thus the scene, in which Léon seduces Emma inside the horse-drawn carriage, captures the movement and violence of the sex act itself, not by describing the act, but by describing the pace of the horse, Léon's angry voice, and the carriage itself with the shades drawn in broad daylight. The reader, unlike the surprised passers-by, has enough information to make him omniscient and from these allusions and these facts he draws the desired conclusion. But the series of "transitions savantes," as Maupassant calls them, with which the author reveals not only the author's point of view but also what is going to happen, are less frequent in Robbe-Grillet's work because these transitions are not and cannot be a function of the character's perception; at least not within Robbe-Grillet's artistic framework.

Since Flaubert is constantly shifting the point of view he can let the reader know (though not Emma) that she will pass through a short happy period by having the sun shine warmly on a wall barometer. After Charles' stupid operation on the boy with the club foot, Emma, in a fit of anger, slams the door, the barometer falls off the wall, breaks, and from then on it will be bad weather for the Bovary "ménage." White bonnets of peasant women are described as "white butterflies." The torn fragments of Emma's letter which Léon throws out the window of the carriage are "white butterflies." The ashes of the wedding bouquet of Charles' first wife which Emma burns in the fireplace are "black butterflies." The alert reader will catch these "transitions savantes" and draw significant inferences from their juxtaposition. Thus the "black butterflies" of morning metamorphose into the ironic "white butterflies" of adultery. There are hundreds of examples like these which only require the patience and ingenuity of the reader to be deciphered. Relating similar aspects of the novel is not unlike solving a puzzle. The clues which Robbe-Grillet accumulates in his novels resemble the hidden transitions of Flaubert or Maupassant. The solution of the puzzle and the tracking down of these clues is not without its measure of aesthetic delight which Flaubert and Robbe-Grillet are both aware of and which, for Maupassant, constitutes one of the highest achievements of the novelist.

In *Une Vie*, for example, Maupassant has described progressive phases of Jeanne's life in such a way as to anticipate, long before they occur, the series of deceptions which will climax her girlish illusions. A typical example might be Jeanne's and her father's purchase of a fish called a "barbue." They carry it home but the weight of the fish exhausts them both. Jeanne's future husband, "un barbu," will "drag her down" and will be a source of endless misery for her.

Flaubert and Maupassant rely primarily on Editorial

Omniscience. James, Joyce, or Faulkner had not yet imposed their narrative restrictions. Since landscape for Flaubert or Maupassant is not necessarily a visual correlative as for Robbe-Grillet (the centipede, for instance), landscapes may be the reflection of a more generalized and pervasive mood. Thus Flaubert surrounds Emma with a world which is in a process of decay or disintegration. Emma makes love to Rodolphe on a bench in the garden which is decaying; every one of her personal contacts will have a comparably decomposed foundation. Flaubert's and Maupassant's Editorial Omniscience need not be pessimistic, which it is. Tolstoy's or Hugo's optimism, for instance, comes through in their work as forcefully as Flaubert's negativism. The events which Maupassant accumulates in order to debilitate Jeanne, and which he labels *Une Vie* (*The Life of a Woman*), suggests the one-sidedness of his own point of view.

Maupassant committed suicide at forty rather than submit to the crippling effects of general paresis while Flaubert, as everyone knows, sought refuge in art because life was too vulgar and too ugly. *Madame Bovary* and *Une Vie*, insomuch as they paint life as a process of decay and deception, reveal their author's points of view. Robbe-Grillet's intrusion is never that personal. His geometric landscapes are intrusions, to be sure, but all we can infer from these descriptions is that the world of objects which surrounds man is *neutral* and that people who anthropomorphize this neutrality are the victims of "tragic complicity." Flaubert's and Maupassant's worlds, though they belong to the domain of the "objective" novel, are biased worlds. They tell us in a thousand different ways, independently of their character's reactions, how awful man's existence on earth is. Robbe-Grillet does not indulge in such biased intrusions because they would not be within his concept of himself as a "scientific" novelist. He is not saying that this is a "good" or a "bad" world but simply that it exists.

There is a logical selectivity in what Mathias sees and does which relates the rigorous determinism of *Le Voyeur* to *Madame Bovary*. The violence of the boat siren at the very beginning of the novel is the first sign that Mathias, like Emma, will be the victim of a compulsive behavior pattern. To argue that the objects precipitate his sexual crime, or that, because of predisposing psychic factors, he chooses to react to objects in a certain way is essentially to look at the same problem from two points of view. Each aspect reinforces the other until it is impossible to distinguish between them. However, it begins with a piece of string and ends with the perverted murder of a thirteen-year-old girl. To argue that the objects "make the crime" as Roland Barthes does [19] shows a curious lack of perception. Nor does the novel deliberately abolish the past as Barthes insists it does. The past is simply visualized as present. Numerous flashbacks reveal that Mathias' psycho-sexual infantilism has its origins in childhood behavior, as, for instance, the reference to bits of string used for games with algae and sea-anemones, "all kinds of complicated and uncertain amusements" (p. 32). In fact, the dominant theme of *Dans le labyrinthe*, that of a child leading a man through the labyrinth of existence, suggests, in the same way as the statuette on Wallas' mantelpiece (child leading a man), that the behavior patterns of Robbe-Grillet's adult protagonists have as their generative source childhood experiences or perhaps in a more general sense *tradition* itself. This means, as Robbe-Grillet states in *Le Monde*, that the novel's protagonist is not a neutral observer: "He is, for example, a sex maniac or a husband whose distrust verges on delirium. And the passions he experiences are so compulsive that they will deform his vision. It is a matter then of a purely subjective description."

What misled a number of critics were Robbe-Grillet's articles in the *NNRF*. In the first, "Une Voie pour le roman futur" (July 1956), he attacked the sacrosanct "analyse psychologique" and critics assumed that, because of the absence of analysis, an inner dimension was lacking in his work. In the second *NNRF* article, "Littérature, Humanisme, Tragédie" (October 1958), Robbe-Grillet, as we have already seen, attacked Sartre and Camus for the anthropomorphic metaphors used by the first person narrator in *L'Etranger* and in *La Nausée*. Other critics, such as Claude Mauriac,[20] were writing facile articles based on Barthes' interpretations and on Robbe-Grillet's early theoretical writings. Robbe-Grillet seems to have taken some delight in deliberately confusing the critics, and it is only recently that he has tried to clarify the issue himself: in an interview published in *Le Monde* (11–17 May 1961), in an article in *Réalitiés* (May 1961), and in an article entitled "Nouveau Roman—Homme Nouveau," which appeared in *La Revue de Paris* (September 1961). His earlier articles, minimizing the importance of the subjectivity in *Le Voyeur* and *La Jalousie*, misled the critics (although Germaine Brée in "New Blinds or Old," *Yale French Studies*, no. 24, and Bruce Morrissette, in *Evergreen*, vol. III, no. 10, 1959, and in *Critique*, July 1959, place *La Jalousie* in its proper perspective).

Le Voyeur has persistently given the critics trouble. Jean Mistler, for instance, considers the novel totally arbitrary.[21] Claude Mauriac states—all evidence in the novel to the contrary notwithstanding—that Robbe-Grillet has retained "everything that is unimportant to the action of the novel which in turn constitutes the novel's very substance." [22] Lagrolet criticized *Le Voyeur* because it gave him the impression of being "an intellectual game without inner necessity," [23] while Maurice Blanchot thinks that it is a book without a center because the murder is not described.[24] Colette Audry assumes that the murder has taken place, but she deduces this from Parts II and III.[25] For Bruno Hahn, this "trou blanc" in the center of the novel indicates that Mathias is suffering from amnesia.[26] And Bernard Dort concludes that Mathias has been forced to follow the "desperate enterprise of a guilty man in search of his innocence," [27] whereas in fact Mathias is merely trying to reconstruct the time sequence of his actions so as to be able to present a logical alibi in case his whereabouts at noon are questioned. Jean Ricardou speaks of "infraconscience" and though he attributes a guilt reaction to Mathias which is not entirely convincing, his article does, nevertheless, point the way to a "subjective" interpretation of Le Voyeur.[28] Justin O'Brien, in his review of the English translation for the New York Times Book Review speaks of the murder as a fait accompli, but Morrissette and Barnes are the only critics who, to my knowledge, dwell on the subjectivity of the novel and who, at the same time, present a logical frame of reference for the murder of Jacqueline.[29]

The variety and scope of interpretations of Le Voyeur lead me to suspect that most readers have not been able to recognize the inner necessity dominating Mathias' compulsive behavior [30] and that, therefore, their attention has focused inevitably on the realism of the detailed descriptions. The objects described are psychic catalysts for Mathias. They are precipitating factors which lead him progressively to the sadistic crime. For example, the constantly recurring figure eight becomes the symbol for his compulsion—the deterministic pattern of his fate—in the same way that the stain of the centipede in La Jalousie ultimately comes to represent the husband's inexorable jealousy.

Robbe-Grillet has constructed Le Voyeur with classical simplicity. Each memory flashback, each fantasy projection, whether conscious or unconscious, has its basis in Mathias' psyche.[31] That Mathias comes upon a string is obviously accidental, but it is significant that he associates it, in a memory flashback, with the bits of string in a shoebox of his boyhood. A chance flying seagull again brings on a memory flashback: as a child he saw a sedentary seagull on the garden piling from his window when he was supposedly doing his homework. Seeing the little girl standing against the dock piling may or may not be accidental; but that his eyes should have selected her from a crowd of dozens of people is, in itself, important. Moreover, that she should be standing in such an awkward position is a distortion of reality comparable in its superimposition to the movie poster in Part II. "Her two hands were behind her, on the small of her back, her legs stiff and slightly apart, her head leaning against the column" (p. 22). Furthermore each time he sees a young girl she will be in some kind of similar position. "Le signe [not *un* but *le*] gravé en forme de huit" is the final precipitating factor for his action. He responds to the figure eight as Pavlov's dog to the bell. He must now act out his compulsion and find a victim for his desire: "in the center of the eight could be seen a reddish exrescence which seemed to be the pivot." The phallic symbolism of the rusty piton is indeed the "pivot," the focal point for Mathias' behavior. It is no longer accidental that he buys candy, or cigarettes (he does not smoke). The string, the candy, and the cigarettes are then part of the necessary pattern. The string must be strong and long enough to tie the victim (there are many reflections on the quality of the string). The candy, as we find out later, is brought to lure the girl. And the burned marks on the dead girl's genitalia, which the islanders mistake for the nibbles of crabs or larger fish, were left by the cigarettes. Mathias' preoccupation with the blue cigarette wrapper floating on the waves is understandable in view of his future purchase of a similar pack, and it is also the beginning of a series of scenes of impending violence whose sexual climax will take place near the cliff at the end of Part I. That Mathias should notice the "slap" of the waves is significant in its association with the raised hand of the male silhouette seen earlier in the morning. "Standing next to the bed and leaning over it slightly was the silhouette of a man with an arm extended towards the ceiling . . . on the night table was a small rectangular object, blue in color—which must have been a pack of cigarettes" (pp. 28–29).

Mathias imagines "the victim"—at this point this is speculation, but for him it is a certainty—to be a young girl. Surely, whether conscious or not, the transition from string to cigarettes to potential girl victim is not gratuitous, but follows a clear-cut pattern of free association. The seagull flying in a figure-eight design reminds him that, as a boy, he drew a similar bird sitting on a thick, rough-hewn pine piling. The seagull of his childhood was

earthbound; all but one gull of his present journey fly.
The seagull of his boyhood is associated with "la tache"
created by a white page. (In *La Jalousie* too, stains—the
centipede on the wall, the oil left by the car on the road
in front of the door, the great red stain that flows down
from the bedroom to the verandah—become objective
correlatives of the husband's jealousy.) The stain of the
white page, however, seems to represent the restraints,
the inhibitions, and the lack of freedom of youth (p. 30).
The figure-eight imprint on the levee, in the center of
which is the piton with its rusty excrescence, has significant
sexual overtones for Mathias. (One shudders to think of
the results if Mathias or the husband were to take a
Rorschach test.) His fascination with the crumpled blue
cigarette wrapper floating on the water and the long detailed descriptions of its motions reveal the importance
Mathias attributes to it. The wrapper—or more precisely
cigarettes—is Mathias' image of violent sexual desire. His
eyes roam selectively and subjectively from the figure eight
to the cigarette wrapper to sensual configurations of sea-
weed revealed when the water recedes from the rocks,
back to the blue paper wrapper which emerges from the
waves with the sound of a slap and is associated with the
blue pack of cigarettes seen that morning in the bedroom
of imminent violence. Figure eights are multiplied in
their associations to include knots on doors, eyeglasses,
cigarette holes in paper, the black holes of eyes, and
presumably the burns on the genitalia of past, present,
and imaginary victims. All of these objects, as Robbe-
Grillet insists, have no inherent symbolism.[32] They are
merely the stimuli which precipitate Mathias' compulsive
desires. Throughout Part I there are innumerable sequences in which Mathias, the salesman, knocks on doors
("frapper"), his ring hitting purposely the space between
the two knotholes. After an imaginary sale at the house
in which Jacqueline lives, Mathias sees the statue of a
woman sculptured in granite, and looking toward the sea.
He concludes, though there is no inscription, that it is
a memorial to the dead, in spite of the fact that it might

as well be a memorial to the fishermen's wives who sit at home and wait for their return.

So far we have an early morning bedroom scene of impending violence, "slapping" waves, Mathias "hitting" doors, a young girl with her arms locked behind her back, a memorial to the dead, and on the village triangle (not square), a poster printed in "violent" colors and featuring a colossus of a man threatening a woman in a long pale chemise. This poster will change three times—three different posters—during the novel and each new poster will represent Mathias' state of mind. The use of the posters is such an effective device that we can hardly blame Robbe-Grillet for using it, in spite of all his theorizing on the neutrality of objects. The first one is violent because Part I is replete with suggestions of sexual violence. The second poster is a landscape which, almost but not entirely, blots out the picture on the first poster underneath. Its ironic title, "Monsieur X sur le double circuit" (p. 165), represents the Mathias of Part II in which he goes through his frenetic time-space reconstructions in order to establish a water-tight alibi. The third poster, in Part III, is white, and as we might suspect by now, it corresponds to Mathias' quietude. The other two posters are no longer visible through the third, so, correspondingly, the "poster" of Mathias' mind no longer superimposes one image upon the other. The pervasive calm of Part III, in addition, is a striking stylistic contrast to the violence of Part I, whose opening lines were: "The boat siren sounded a second time, a sharp prolonged whistle, followed by three rapid blasts, with a violence strong enough to shatter eardrums—a violence without purpose and which remained without result."

The plot, which revolves around the murder of the thirteen-year-old girl, Jacqueline, is not a tale told by an idiot,[33] but visualized by a "sex maniac." The novel is full of "violence sans objet" since the murderer, Mathias, has no "reasonable" motive for his crime. Because no one suspects the violence of his compulsion he is not apprehended. As Bruno Hahn demonstrates in an excellent article,[34] only those islanders are suspect who are thought to have had a motive. It is ironic that so many readers, like the islanders, do not suspect Mathias either. Therefore, his crime is "sans résultat" because, contrary to the traditional detective novel, the guilty person in Le Voyeur is not caught and does not atone for his offense against society. The boat siren (the double-meaning of this word should not pass unnoticed), coming as it does after the initial "it was as though no one had heard," is a signal, a warning, and one of the very few sounds—since Robbe-Grillet's novels are almost entirely visual—which we find in this work. It is the sign that Mathias will be caught in the mesh of his psychosexual infantilism, that the island of his birth will be a trap: "midst the nets and the traps . . . Mathias could not walk as quickly as he might have wished" (p. 38).

Subsequently Mathias will notice a dismembered doll in the lower corner of the movie poster, later associated with a barmaid who is described as "an articulated doll" (p. 64); then he sees some severed crabs' legs. The crabs, like the centipede in La Jalousie, become hauntingly obsessive. Mathias stops at a bar where the eyes of the waitress are like those of a "sleeping doll"; "Her skin is fragile" (p. 57). The café owner, who bears a striking resemblance to the man on the movie poster, menaces the waitress. The drinking sailors say that she needs to be slapped (associated with the "slap" of the waves, and implying that Jacqueline will be slapped before she is subdued). "The Whip!" shouts someone. Mathias then sees, imagines, remembers, projects (which?) the image of the waitress putting her hands behind her back, like the girl on the poster, like the girl on the dock, like Violette, like Jacqueline (which?). "Are you asleep?" says the café owner belligerently to the waitress. This phrase provides a kind of hypnotic reinforcement to the way in which Mathias passes freely from reality to fantasy. "There is in the spoken word," says Robbe-Grillet, "a solid, monstrous, definitive *presence* which separates it radically from all thought." [35]

And indeed Mathias' dislocation of reality corresponds to similar dislocations which occur in dreams, to the incongruous juxtaposition and superimposition of objects. When Mathias goes to the bedroom above the bar to sell Monsieur Robbin's wife a watch, he "sees" the bed and the draperies (like those on the movie poster) in a state of turmoil, as if a struggle had taken place. The night table with the package of blue cigarettes on it (like the one seen previously) is obviously rich in associations which the alert reader must make in order to follow Mathias through his psychic contortions. The whole atmosphere is now loaded with sexuality and violence. The memorial "to the dead" reminds Mathias that he has forgotten to buy cigarettes (for what purpose, since he does not smoke?). The reader must then associate death, cigarettes, and intended victim. A fish in a store is seen as a long dagger. A window display model is "the body of a young woman with severed arms and legs" (p. 71). The dark alleys and cluttered stairways through which he passes are the objective descriptions of his festering mind: "Dark corridors with closed doors, narrow frustrating stairs, he lost himself once more midst these [ses] phantoms" (p. 73).

Since no detail is extraneous, and *Le Voyeur* is a study of Mathias' psychic behavior, the associations of his mind are free to roam in the past as memory or in the future as daydreaming or in the present, either as reality or as a hypnotic dream-state. "It is this mental time which interests us, with its strange attributes, its gaps, its obsessions, its obscure regions, because this mental *time* relates our passions and our life" (*Réalités*, p. 96). Mathias' affective state then becomes a composite of memory and imagination. It combines fragments of scenes experienced with fragments of projected possibilities which are "seen" together in a dream-like present: "The giant's hand moves slowly towards the fragile base of her neck where it comes to rest. The hand molds itself around the neck, presses down without apparent effort, but with such persuasive force that it forces her weak body to give way, slowly.

Bending her legs the girl draws back one foot, then the other, and of her own accord kneels on the flagstones" (p. 77).

Here, Mathias is animating the poster with a blend of reality and fantasy in order to form the composite image of his inner vision. He then animates a newspaper article in the same way, with fragments of a past experience, or perhaps merely of his imagination. Everything, however, is seen taking place in the present: "her small obedient hands move upward along her thighs, pass behind her hips and come to rest finally slightly below the small of the back—fists crossed—as though captive" (p. 77). Her big dark eyes have eyelashes like a doll's, then "a stronger wave hit against the rock with the sound of a slap" (p. 77). Soon afterwards, reference to the bicycle as a "belle machine" sends Mathias' eye roving again up and down the movie poster and casts his imagination into a swirl of erotic fantasy which is finally interrupted by the voice of the bicycle mechanic. Mathias gets on his bicycle and takes the road to the lighthouse (phallic symbol?). It is hardly accidental that Jacqueline's house—that girl whom Mathias knows to be a "real demon"—should be in the same direction. Jacqueline is not at home, but a photograph of her reminds Mathias of Violette (viol-ette, or little rape, the diminutive used because of her age). Subsequently Jacqueline will be Violette-Jacqueline for him. Mathias "sees" her "sitting against the rectilinear trunk of a pine tree [the seagull of his boyhood was drawn sitting on a pine piling], her head on the bark, her legs stiff and slightly spread, her arms pulled behind her back. Her position, an equivocal mélange of abandon and constraint, might lead one to surmise that she had been tied to a tree [with one of Mathias' strings?]" (p. 83).

This composite image, the construction of his present desire with the images of a past or imaginary encounter (similar in process to the "imagination" of the movie poster), blends directly with the mother's story describing how Jacqueline, who has "le démon au corps cette gamine!" (p. 85), had her picture taken the year before. In earlier times, the daughter would have been burned as a witch, says the mother, and immediately Mathias' hypersensitive imagination sends erotic flames licking around her and the pine tree to which she is tied. As soon as he finds out that Jacqueline is guarding her sheep "by the edge of the cliff, far from the road" (p. 86), he leaves instantly. He is so eager to find her that he pedals his bicycle faster and faster, begins to perspire, and misses two easy watch sales for lack of concentration: "he was in such a hurry to leave that he had the impression of having missed the sale simply for not having stayed ten more seconds" (p. 86). He soon finds himself near the lighthouse. The Marek farm is to the left of the road (if he were selling watches, he should have stopped there, since it is the only house in the vicinity), but Mathias takes the path to the right. "After several hundred meters, the ground slopes gently towards the first undulations of the cliff. Mathias need only let himself go" (p. 87). This bicycle ride down the undulating slope towards the ocean marks the end of Part I. It is a simultaneous release of tension, stylistic as well as sexual. Previous past tense verbs suddenly focus on the present "il n'a plus qu'à se laisser descendre." The event for which all of Part I has been preparing us is about to take place. Moreover, a careful reading of Part I would have left no doubts as to the outcome of this scene.

With the beginning of Part II, Mathias is back at the road intersection. It is the intervening lapse of time which so many critics have described as a "trou" (a hole) in the story, or a story without a center. We have been forced to visualize the young girl with her legs apart and her hands behind her back for the last one hundred pages. All the details and all the clues have been meticulously provided, and, if we have followed Mathias' psychic evolution, a realistic description of the crime becomes superfluous and would be, in itself, an anticlimax.

In Part II Mathias is no longer in a hurry. The description of the long shadow cast by the stone kilometer marker on the road indicates that Mathias' eye is lingering on its suggestive contours. He also notices nearby the crushed cadaver of a small frog, "thighs spread, arms in the form of a cross" (p. 91), and its relationship to the elongated shadow no doubt explains his fascination for the juxtaposition. Does it not represent a scene in which he has just taken part (a shadow phallus and a corpse)? It is also our first clue that Jacqueline is dead. The shadow of the kilometer marker then blends into the larger contours of a cloud which slowly masks the sun. Mathias "sees" a flying frog which metamorphoses into a seagull overhead and which passes over the tip of a telephone pole. His eyes then return to the path on which the shadows of the telephone wires are no longer visible. These are all details, which, now that Mathias' sexual compulsion has been satisfied, he has time to register, whereas, in his initial haste, he had time only to observe the distance on the kilometer marker. The urgency of his pedalling to find Jacqueline-Violette climaxed his sexual compulsion. The violence of his desire meant that he "had eyes" only for the satisfaction of his maniacal drive. Now that the sadistic, perverted crime has assuaged his need, he is no longer in a hurry, and therefore, his consciousness registers details which it was previously "blind" to, and which, more importantly, help to define his crime for the reader.

Then, he sees a peasant woman no more than fifty meters away, and because of a sense of guilt, he pretends to be fixing a bicycle chain which is not in need of repair. He seems now to have a grasp on reality. The sight of the peasant woman brings him out of his daze, and he will henceforth devote all his efforts to the creation of a plausible alibi. Part III, corresponding to the blank third poster, is full of calm and waiting, in spite of several compulsive leads. Finally, Mathias boards the boat and leaves the island, unapprehended.

In conclusion then, we can say that Robbe-Grillet is initiating a new naturalism based on Freudian determinism. If this is an "age of suspicion," as Nathalie Sarraute

claims it is, then only a narrative caught under the objectivism of a literary microscope can satisfy the reader's
"souci" for the truth. The feeble-minded Marek son who
witnessed the crime is, as Morrissette says,[36] a voyeur,
but only in a minor sense. The real voyeur is Mathias or
perhaps even the reader who "sees" the crime happening
long before it has occurred. The original title of the book,
Le Voyageur is, in this sense, relevant and suggestive.
Le Voyageur focuses all our attention on Mathias. *Le
Voyeur* generalizes the meaning of the novel and expands
the point of view. There are in reality three voyeurs: the
Marek son who fails to grasp the significance of what he
has seen: Mathias who visualizes the crime in his mind's
eye; and the reader who "sees" through the window of
Robbe-Grillet's novel. Robbe-Grillet is in this sense and,
contrary to Champigny's assertion,[37] a spiritual descendant of Rimbaud. Within this "scientific" novel
of his he has created synthetic hallucinations by projecting the "inner film" of Mathias" deranged senses.
Mathias, ironically, is not a *voyant*, but just a voyeur,
insomuch as he never grasps the meaning of his visions
(the hallucinations of the mentally ill are as "real" as
reality is for those of us who are "normal"). The real
voyant is Robbe-Grillet who has devised this "long and
reasoned derangement." We, the readers, can then "see"
with the eyes (hence the emphasis within the novel on
holes, glasses, and the multiplicity of figure eights which
resemble eyes) of the protagonist, whether he is a jealous
husband, a "sex maniac," or a man caught in the labyrinth
of his dreams and his fever. And we must decipher the
meaning of these hallucinations (juxtaposition and superimposition of images) if we are to understand Robbe-
Grillet's apparently "objective" novels; if we are to see
the truth. His attack on psychological analysis in reality
masks an intense fascination with the working of the
mind, insomuch as his novels are the re-creation of a
subjective world. It is the reader who, through the effort of
his participation, is the analyst, and, by virtue of his insight into the projected images of things, sees and under-

stands the mechanism of the protagonist's mind. The title then applies to the inner optics of the novel, the simultaneous relationship between Mathias' psyche and the author's technique. Robbe-Grillet's technique *is* the way Mathias' mind works. The whole—form and content —summed up perfectly in one word: *Voyeur*.

IN THE 1933 PREFACE to the French translation of *Sanctuary* Malraux says that this novel represents the "intrusion of Greek tragedy in the detective story." Robbe-Grillet's first published novel, *Les Gommes* (*The Gum Erasers*, 1953),[1] seems to be a deliberately contrived rendition, not of *Sanctuary* but of Malraux' famous pronouncement. I hasten to add, however, that Faulkner's influence is not negligible since Robbe-Grillet's work reveals similar preoccupations with time, point of view, and objectivized subjectivity. *Sanctuary* is, as Malraux tells us, a novel with a detective-story atmosphere but without detectives, while *Les Gommes*, on the contrary (and at least superficially), has the stereotyped victim-assassin-detective relationship.

The force of destiny, however, relates these two otherwise dissimilar books. Popeye is hanged for a crime he did not commit while Goodwin is burned for Popeye's crime. Wallas becomes the assassin in spite of his efforts to resolve an alleged murder. Temple Drake's progression from rape to whore-house to nymphomania is an elaboration of her own destiny as a function of character. Wallas' Oedipus complex must, I suppose, be interpreted as a function of character. These are not, in the Greek sense, destinies imposed by the gods. Temple is, we infer from her deliberate flaunting of parental and school rules, reacting to the rigid authoritarianism of her father. But this revolt, like Wallas' search, remains on a subconscious level. She is rebelling against the principles which a self-righteous Baptist community tries to inculcate in her, not through reason, but through arbitrary discipline. Her tragedy, if we may call it that, is in not having understood and resolved the reasons for her revolt. "I told you this was going to happen," is a cry of partial awareness over the "inevitable" consequences of her behavior. Popeye's tragedy, as Faulkner tries to show at the end of the book, belongs, like Temple's, to a psychological domain. Though there is the hint of a congenital defect he is suffering from the trauma of a broken home, neglect, and maladjusted parents—derivative factors, which stem, as Faulkner implies, from various levels of social inequity.

The action of the story depends for its elaboration on the chance encounter of people and the triggering of latent behavior possibilities as a result of this fateful bringing together of certain personality types. *Sanctuary*, like Greek tragedy, depends on the relationship between people and a religious tradition (in this case the decadence of Christianity) but unlike Greek tragedy we no longer interpret the behavior of personages as injury to the gods, unless by gods we mean an offense against the self or against society. We could, no doubt, equate biological determinism (if we could ever measure its effect on behavior) with the governing role the gods played in Greek culture, but a hero's fatal flaw, in the light of modern psychology is, perhaps, not as irrevocable as it once was in Greek tragedy.

In *Les Gommes*, Wallas, a detective, has been assigned to solve the alleged murder of Daniel Dupont. Wallas does not know what the reader knows: that Dupont is not dead. Wallas asks questions, follows clues (which seem unrelated to the crime), and after twenty-four hours of walking through the labyrinthine streets of a city in Northern Europe (with swollen feet—*Oedipus* in Greek) he shoots the presumed assassin only to discover that he, Wallas, has become the murderer of Daniel Dupont. This is a parody of Greek tragedy as well as of the traditional detective novel. The novel operates on two more levels, however, both of these serious. If we, as readers, follow the clues so meticulously provided, we discover that Wallas shoots Dupont (his father) because he has not resolved his Oedipus complex.[2] Destiny has been given a bright shiny Freudian veneer. The multiplicity of the points of view, most of them contradictory, adds a social dimension which is also to be taken seriously. But this novel is a reversal of the standard concept of the detective story and Wallas discovers, ironically, that all the clues he was following have only led him, the would-be-savior, to murder. His destiny is therefore directed by the apparently irrevocable compulsion of an unresolved Oedipus complex. As in *Sanctuary* we witness the intrusion of Greek tragedy in the detective novel but with one important distinction: *Les Gommes* is a parody whereas *Sanctuary* is not. Destiny, we might add, is the complexity of events unleashed by a multiplicity of factors: time, historical and social coincidence, and the manifestations of the self caught in the labyrinth of time and place.

The interest in the detective story, as W. H. Auden points out in an article entitled "The Guilty Vicarage," stems from the dialectic of innocence and guilt: "in the Aristotelian description of tragedy there is Concealment (the innocent seem guilty and the guilty seem innocent) and Manifestation (the real guilt is brought to consciousness)."[3] *Les Gommes* resembles Greek tragedy in that the readers (audience) know the truth while the personages (actors) do not. The irony of the novel is that Wallas thinks himself innocent until his guilt is brought to consciousness, a revelation which is as surprising to the reader as it is to Wallas. Unlike the real whodunit in which a murder occurs at the beginning and the reader is kept in suspense until the resolution of guilt and innocence, the murder, in *Les Gommes*, occurs at the end. It is the murder itself which casts light on the activities of the detective rather than vice versa.

In Greek tragedy and in the detective story the characters are not changed in or by their actions. In Greek tragedy their actions are fated and in the detective story the irrevocability of death—the mysterious circumstances surrounding the appearance of a corpse—also fates action. In *Les Gommes* the reversal of detective story procedure casts such a strong light on Wallas' activities that it forces insight and thereby implies the possibility of altering behavior. This murder is the bringing to consciousness of an Oedipus complex which, until the end, has remained unconscious. Unlike the stereotyped detective novel which is primarily "escape" reading, *Les Gommes* suggests the possibility of change and thereby brings this work within the domain of literature.

In all of Robbe-Grillet's novels the potential for change is not a function of the character's insight into his behavior pattern but depends on the reader's insight into the nature and causes of "tragedy." Thus, with the exception of the narrator in *Dans le labyrinthe*, none of Robbe-Grillet's personages achieves insight into his or her personal problems or into the larger dilemma of the human situation. This is, in fact, their "tragedy." Like Tess anthropomorphizing the world around her in terms of her suicidal impulses, Wallas projects his Oedipus complex into cityscape details, Mathias selects objects from his material environment which correspond to his latent sexuality and violence, the jealous husband sees his physical surroundings through the eyes of jealousy, and A in *Marienbad* finds herself trapped by a decor whose neutrality, like hers, has been violated and infused with human meaning. This is the theme that runs through all of Robbe-Grillet's novels. Meursault speaks of the world's indifference to man. Camus and Sartre, when speaking for themselves, refer to the world as "absurd." But the world, says Robbe-Grillet is neither indifferent nor absurd. It exists, that is all. It is simply *there*. To say that the world is *indifferent* is to anthropomorphize it, to give it volition. To say that the world is *absurd* is to project one's own sense of tragic mortality into the chemical and physical composition of matter which, from all appearances, does not care or react to man's metaphysical anguish. Robbe-Grillet calls this absence of reaction *neutrality*. But matter loses its neutrality the moment man begins to talk about it. And so we speak of *welcome* dawns, *hostile* nights, and *green* banana groves, not because the dawn or the night or the grove care or could react to these attributes but because of human associations, experience, and language.

Robbe-Grillet has therefore eliminated the anthropomorphic adjective because it says nothing about the material environment but does say everything about the perceiver. We might think that the anthropomorphic adjective would help his cause, but apparently not. By eliminating it and by forcing the reader's attention on the geometric linear surface of objects Robbe-Grillet has tried to communicate the neutrality of objects. All his novels, however, are examples of the violation of this neutrality. His characters do indeed behave like "sick animals." Wallas shoots his father, Mathias kills Jacqueline, the husband is delirious, and A is on the verge of madness. All of these people are enmeshed in the determinism of a tragic complicity which is of their own making. Robbe-Grillet's novels demonstrate the tragic nature of the "pathetic fallacy." None of his characters are even remotely conscious of what is happening to them. The only exceptions would be X in *Marienbad* who, because he contrives the experiment for A, seems to know what he is doing; the doctor-Robbe-Grillet-narrator of *Dans le labyrinthe* who, for obvious reasons understands the nature of "tragic complicity;" and, though it is not likely, Wallas. It does not seem probable that Wallas understands the nature of the Oedipus clues provided for him by the author. It does not seem likely that many readers will either. Yet the meaning of the novel hinges on an explication of the Oedipus problem. Without this insight the novel has no cohesion—it lacks a center. So the possibility for change is primarily the reader's. The reader will, if he understands the novels, and if he disapproves of murder, understand how Wallas' and Mathias' homicide was triggered as a result of their complicity with their environment. So perhaps unpremeditated murder is avoidable, and madness along with it. Jealousy seems less subject to control though *La Jalousie* demonstrates obsessional qualities with clinical accuracy. If change is possible it will depend on insight into and the resolution of "tragic complicity." Since this seems to be the "raison d'être" of Robbe-Grillet's novels they are not, in fact, mere detective stories.

Destiny then becomes a function of "character" as well as of chance and depends on the right fortuitous (and possible if not probable) encounter between people, things, and events. If change is possible, it will not be manifest until the very end, until the reasons or the need for change have been exposed. If the reader understands how and why Robbe-Grillet's characters behave and if he judges their behavior he will, one hopes, relearn to see the world—and will thereby himself avoid the type of behavior which can result from anthropomorphizing it. If an unresolved Oedipus complex affects behavior, as *Les Gommes* so strongly implies, then its resolution will eliminate all those factors of destiny which control behavior and which are unpredictable. When critics speak of character as destiny do they not have in mind the unconscious and therefore uncontrollable factors of one's personality makeup which influence behavior in strange and unforeseen ways? To bring these factors to consciousness is perhaps the first step towards controlling them. This, it seems to me, is what Robbe-Grillet's novels are doing. Technically they objectify the subconsious. Morally they are asking the reader to understand the insidious ways of unconsciously anthropomorphizing nature. This is why Robbe-Grillet does not use the anthropomorphic adjective so typical of Roquentin's and Meursault's perceptions. The adjective, as Camus' and Sartre's novels demonstrate, renders the process conscious or at least semiconscious. Robbe-Grillet's characters behave as though they were unconscious of the stimuli which influence their actions. They are the victims of the deterministic nature of their compulsions. Their fate is inextricably linked with their obsession and they act out their destiny.

To understand how this process works is to be able to change and insomuch as Robbe-Grillet wants to eliminate "tragedy," as he defines it, he must first reveal the invisible mechanics of the process. He has in fact explained how the subconscious works, and how it selects specific details for the satisfaction of its needs by projecting the subconscious' selectivity onto visually described details of the environment.

In Greek tragedy fate was inevitable. Man's fatal flaw led him irrevocably to perform the act which destiny had willed. The modern concept of man is perhaps less deterministic. We believe that the resolution of the fatal flaw (the Oedipus complex for instance) can lead to insight, the alteration of behavior patterns, and change. This, it seems to me, is the difference between Greek tragedy and modern tragedy. This is, in fact, one of Freud's great contributions to modern thought. The Freudian nature of *Les Gommes* reinforces the hypothesis of impending change. I should stress, perhaps, how *Les Gommes* illustrates the fundamental theme of the modern novel as a search. Jacques Revel's search for self in Butor's *Emploi du temps* is comparable to the search Wallas is engaged in. The fundamental difference between these two novels, however, is that in Butor's novel Jacques Revel performs the search for the reader, whereas in *Les Gommes* the reader performs the search for Wallas. This is what I mean by reader involvement or reader participation. The reader must solve the problem for the character in the novel and in so doing (as he must if he is to understand the novel) he can assimilate the experience of a specific novel, generalize it, and make it part of his insight into living. If he does this he will have made the first step towards eliminating "tragedy."

And so, within the context of *Les Gommes*, Wallas' actions are fated like Oedipus' in Sophocle's *Oedipus the King*: Oedipus was abandoned to die by his parents while Wallas is the son of a father he has never known. Establishing such parallels is essential for the proper elucidation of the novel and, appropriately enough, Robbe-Grillet has provided the reader with the necessary legendary clues which will guide him and Wallas during the search. Behind the superficiality of a detective story lurks the deeper meaning of a search for self: "The machinery, perfectly regulated, cannot occasion the least surprise. One need only follow the text, reciting sentence after sentence, and the word will be realized." [4]

Wallas' watch has stopped, symbolically, at 7:30 P.M., the time of Garinati's attempted assassination of Daniel Dupont. It will resume ticking again twenty-four hours later immediately after Dupont's real death. There is, in addition to this formal unity of time, the cessation of clock time and the expansion, for Wallas, of human time. It will be during this hiatus that Wallas will relive all the mythological implications of his Oedipus complex. The jacket of the first edition of *Les Gommes* says that it is "the story of the twenty-four hours which elapse between the pistol shot and the death, the time it has taken the bullet to travel three or four meters—a hiatus of twenty-four hours." This stopping of time is comparable to Quentin's act (in *The Sound and the Fury*) of breaking the hands off the dial of his watch. This action has symbolic value because it forces us to see time without the help of mechanical aids. "Time is dead as long as it is being clicked off by little wheels," says Quentin; "only when the clock stops does time come to life." [5] *Les Gommes* concerns itself with the evolution of Wallas' psychological time. This inner time of his explains and gives meaning to the search in spite of the constant imposition of apparently irrelevant details. As in the printed text on the three yellow street posters there will be in the novel "here and there, as a beacon, terms which are suspect" (p. 53), which the reader must catch and combine with other similar clues in order to form the picture of total insight.

Early in the course of his peregrinations Wallas remembers that, as a child, he had visited this same city: "He remembers the image of a dead-end canal section; tied to one of the wharves is an old boat no longer in use—the remains of a sailing ship? A very low stone bridge bars the entrance. It was probably not exactly like that: the boat would not have been able to pass under the bridge. Wallas resumes his way back into the city" (p. 46).

This passage is typical of Robbe-Grillet's use of form as a function of content (or vice-versa). The dead-end street and the remains of a sailing vessel will be symbolic of Wallas' arrested emotional development. The city, with its Circular Boulevard, its canals, and its streets will be the exteriorized image of Wallas' psyche. As he moves through time and space towards the resolution of the enigma, that is, towards the "rue des Arpenteurs" where the murder is going to occur, as well as towards the inner city of his subconscious, his attention will focus (as does Mathias' in *Le Voyeur*) on details which will be the objective correlatives of his dilemma. Garinati (Wallas' double) will therefore see "a fabulous animal: the head, the neck, the chest, the front paws, the body of a lion with its long tail and the wings of an eagle" (p. 37) in the débris of corks and pieces of wood floating on the survace of a canal. This is, is it not, a description of the sphinx? But unlike *Le Voyeur*, in which virtually all landscape is a function of Mathias' character, Robbe-Grillet does not make all clues dependent on Wallas' perception. He uses, instead, the device of double identity—either between Wallas and the other assassin, Garinati (who wears a similar raincoat and whose attention, like Wallas', focuses on the paperweight on Dupont's desk), or in the physical resemblance between Wallas and the new assassin of a new Dupont victim (this time Albert Dupont). The initials of the new assassin, V. S., resemble and sound like the French pronunciation of Wallas.

Robbe-Grillet has given us the literary equivalent of a Freudian interpretation of the Oedipus myth—the subconscious hostility of the child who would like to kill his father and sleep with his mother. The drunkard who pesters the clients of the café with his riddles provides the appropriate clue when he, like the Sphinx, asks what animal is parricidal in the morning, incestuous at noon,

and blind in the evening (p. 234). Wallas, who has no
insight into his "complex," is therefore "blind" when he
(like Oedipus) decides to solve the mystery. He covets his
stepmother at noon in the Victor-Hugo stationery store,
and in the evening he shoots his father. In the mean-
time his attention focuses on a decor which will reveal
the parallel between this modern detective story and the
ancient Oedipus myth. He notices the design of a curtain
on which two shepherds are giving sheep's milk to a small
naked infant (p. 50). As his search continues he comes to
a square in the center of which he sees "a bronze configuration representing a Greek chariot being drawn by
two horses. In the chariot are several personages, probably
symbolic" (p. 62), one of whom is, no doubt, Laius,
Oedipus' father. Wallas then buys a newspaper in which
the following headline catches his attention: "Severe
traffic accident on Delphi road" (p. 64). It was in his
chariot, on the road to Delphi that Laius, kind of Thebes,
tried to force Oedipus from the road and was slain by the
young man. It was the oracle of Delphi which later announced that the scourges ravaging the land would not
cease until the Thebans had driven the unknown murderer
of Laius out of the country. Oedipus, after having offered
ritual maledictions against the assassin, undertook, detective fashion, to find out who the assassin really was. His
inquiries (like Wallas') finally led to the discovery that
the guilty man was none other than himself, and that
Jocasta, whom he had married, was his mother.

Opposite the statue of the symbolic bronze figures described in *Les Gommes* is the significantly suggestive
"avenue de la Reine." Wallas then asks for the best way
to reach the "rue de Corinthe." It was Polybus, King of
Corinth, who, after the shepherd had brought the foundling to him, adopted him and named him Oedipus because
of his hurt and swollen feet. As Wallas passes once more
by the bronze statue he reads the inscription on the base:
"Le Char de l'Etat" (p. 85). After Wallas covets a young
girl (perhaps his sister) in a stationery store he goes to
Dupont's apartment where he takes Dupont's revolver

(p. 95), an appropriate phallic symbol. By this symbolic
act Wallas negates his father's sexual potential. The theme
of the foundling child reappears more frequently now—
on the curtains (p. 108) and in the drunkard's monologue
(p. 121). The pace of the novel quickens. In the display
window of the Victor Hugo stationery store Wallas sees
a mannequin painting "a hill on which, midst cypresses,
loom the ruins of a Greek temple; . . . But in front of
the man, instead of the Hellenic countryside, rises, by way
of a setting, an immense photographic print of a city
intersection of the twentieth century. The quality of this
picture and its clever arrangement give an all the more
striking reality to the landscape, insomuch as it is the
negation of the drawing which is supposed to reproduce it"
(p. 131).

Wallas recognizes the picture as the front of the hotel
of the "rue des Arpenteurs," where Dupont was alleged
to have been murdered. This description, and another
similar one, firmly establish the reciprocity of the Greek
and the modern landscapes. This exchange of a mythical
and historical decor for a contemporary setting reinforces
the theme of the book. The woman in the stationery
store (Dupont's ex-wife) informs him that the picture is
of the ruins of Thebes. It was Creon, who had governed
Thebes since the death of Laius, who promised the crown
and the hand of Jocasta to the man who could deliver the
city from the scourge which had been ravaging the land.
The scourge ravaging this Northern City is a political
plot which has assassinated nine people in nine days.
Oedipus delivers the city, then marries his mother. Wallas
does not actually sleep with the proprietress of the stationery store but there is an aroused sexual interest due
to her very presence there with him—"with her cooing
laughter, which seems to come from her whole body . . .
Provocative and tantalizing . . . His wife" (p. 187).
Wallas' imagination then blends the memory of his
mother ("the door closes and she, the all too sensuous
wife, is there in the bedroom," p. 187) with the image of
Dupont's divorced spouse. Wallas then imagines killing

Dupont (p. 188). This will be a surrealistic prefiguration of the actual murder, and a typical Freudian wish-fulfillment.

Events run their course because Wallas has followed the irrevocable pattern of his unresolved Oedipus complex. As in Greek tragedy the novel is divided into five chapters (acts) with a prologue and an epilogue, and as we read this Freudian version of the Oedipus legend it seems clear that *Les Gommes*, even more than *Sanctuary*, represents the intrusion of Greek tragedy in the detective novel. The mystery has been solved, human time has run its course and, appropriately enough, the revolver shot activates Wallas' watch twenty-four hours later at the exact time it had stopped. Mechanical time can now take over again, the bullet has run its course, and destiny has been fulfilled.

As Wallas' diurnal activities lead him from canal to street, to Circular Boulevard, to the Court House, to the Post Office, to the "rue des Arpenteurs," and to several stationery stores it becomes clear that he is looking for a certain brand of eraser with very specific textural characteristics (p. 132):

> A soft, light, crumbly eraser which is not deformed by crushing but is pulverized; an eraser which is easily broken into sections which are, in turn, as smooth and shiny as mother of pearl. He remembers seeing one once . . . at a friend's house. . . . It had the form of a yellowish two to three centimeter cube with slightly rounded edges—perhaps from use. The trademark was printed on one of the sides, but too faint to be still readable: you could only decipher the two middle letters "di"; there must have been at least two letters in front and two more behind.

This eraser, like the figure eight for Mathias and the centipede for the jealous husband, is the objectification of Wallas' problem and gives the title to the novel. We need only add "Oe——pe" to the two middle letters "di" to get *Oedipe*. Now we realize why it was so important for Wallas to find this particular eraser. This is his complex and therefore no other eraser will do. Mathias, in *Le Voyeur*, returns to the island of his childhood where he will commit murder. Wallas too will be caught inextricably in a chain of events which will not lead him to solve Dupont's assassination but to perpetrate it. Wallas finds himself propelled towards the inevitable climax which will be the resolution of his drama.

The particular succession and configuration of objects and events within this Northern city will, once again, lead the protagonist astray. Just as A in *Marienbad* loses herself in the formal gardens of the "chateau" (much to X's astonishment) or the sick and tired soldier loses his way in the labyrinth of a strange city, so also Wallas loses himself in a labyrinth which, in one sense, is of his own making but which, in a larger context (his unresolved Oedipus complex) is an expression of the forces of destiny. We conclude then that every person will give symbolic value to those particular objects which, in answer to a deep-seated psychological affinity, will evoke a response in the perceiver. It need not be conscious. In fact, the more unconscious it is the more insidious the rapport, since then, the objects which are in themselves "neutral," as Robbe-Grillet says, act as our outside catalysts, or destiny, and lead us to surprising consequences—at least at surprising as Wallas' astonishment at having shot his father without premeditation. Wallas is trying to recollect events which "the gum erasers" have symbolically effaced. The novel is not a process of tearing down but of building up. The right eraser which, with the passage of time, seems to have obscured the edges of remembrance, will be the essential clue for the construction of total insight.

In this first novel Robbe-Grillet has begun to explore the possibilities of "tragic complicity." The results are interesting but not totally satisfying. I have purposely limited my analysis to a linear elucidation of the Oedipus problem. Actually the novel is a complex proliferation of events, incidents, and points of view. Like *Les Faux-Monnayeurs* it is more interesting theoretically than successful artistically. Like Gide, Robbe-Grillet has tried to write a dense novel with multiple facets and, like Gide again, he does not quite bring it off. It is too diffuse, it lacks focus and, although solving the Oedipus cycle is absorbing for a time, it is hardly worth the effort. Robbe-Grillet appears to have sensed this problem because in his subsequent novels he has limited the point of view and eliminated peripheral material. In doing this he has written works which are closer to the "récit" than to the novel. If *La Porte étroite* is a "récit," what are *La Jalousie* or *L'Etranger* which are, nevertheless, called novels? Perhaps the term novel, as Northrop Frye suggests, should be saved for more complex interrelationships between people as in James's novels or in parts of Proust's work.[6]

This is what seems to be the matter with *Les Gommes*. It has, as its central focus, the resolution of Wallas' Oedipus complex. But the reader's attention is dispersed, directed towards other irrelevant relationships which are not justified. Since the reader already knows that Daniel Dupont is not dead the conflicting hypotheses concerning this event do not reinforce the main theme. They do point out, however, the extreme subjectivity of every point of view and the possibility of error due either to lack of information, or to misinformation.[7] If Robbe-Grillet has tried to give us a multifaceted equivalent of *As I Lay Dying* he does not succeed because, unlike Faulkner's work, in which every point of view illuminates the central problem of the novel, the hypotheses of the detective Laurent, the reactions of the assassin Garinati, Bona's political plot, Dr. Juard's concealment of the crime are unrelated to Oedipus, and become merely a part of the traditional framework of the detective story—there to confuse the reader yet maintain his interest. Since the reader knows that Dupont is not dead, all this subterfuge is unnecessary. *Le Voyeur*, by eliminating all that is unessential is a stronger work of art and, by contrast, reveals the deficiencies of *Les Gommes*.

Both novels have as their central theme the exploration of a human psyche as it contaminates and as it is in turn contaminated by "reality." But the inner necessity governing *Le Voyeur* and *La Jalousie* are not present in *Les Gommes*. Wallas' search, like the detective story which it parodies, is an intellectual game. The reader is amused, fascinated, and delighted as he isolates a particular set of details from a vast array of false clues supplied in order to distract and confuse him. *Les Gommes* like many of Hitchcock's films (*Vertigo* for instance) is airtight in its verisimilitude until the very end. At the end the structure of the film collapses and the viewer becomes conscious of the fact that he has been deceived—that certain details were deliberately withheld or that a false lead was surreptitiously provided in lieu of the truth. *Les Gommes*, of course, does not fall apart as *Vertigo* does in spite of the arbitrary materials from which the plot is woven. It is perhaps sufficient to point out that in *Les Gommes* Robbe-Grillet is beginning to explore the inherent possibilities of "tragic complicity."

5   *IN THE LABYRINTH*

THINGS WHICH ARE DESCRIBED geometrically "relate only to
themselves, with no chinks or crevices for us to slip into,
and without causing us the least dizziness" ("Nature,
Humanisme, Tragédie"). This is the key to Robbe-
Grillet's work and *Dans le labyrinthe* is no exception.
As in *La Jalousie*, each time the narrator's attention moves
from a purely geometric description to color, the imagination whirls off into space in a series of associations induced
by the chinks and crevices which it has slipped into. The
red curtains of the doctor-narrator's room remind him of
the red curtains of the room in which the soldier died. It
is this color red (blood? life?) which is the immediate
stimulus for the subsequent fictional narrative. In the
solitude and silence of his room, as he contemplates the
contents of the box, the table, the lamp, the mirror, the
picture, the dresser, etc. his imagination "contaminates"
these objects, relates them to the death of the soldier,
and his dream carries him into a fictional world where
rational laws of time and space give way to the irrational
impulses of a surreal experience. The effect is cyclical:
our attention goes from table, to lamp, to fly, to curtains,
to snow, to street lamp, to soldier, to box, and back to the
table, the crack, the picture, the box, its contents on the
table, the dust, the snow, the cold, the soldier, the boy
leading the soldier, the boy in the picture holding the box,
etc., in a series of labyrinthine associations through which
we retrace not only the soldier's peregrinations through

the streets of the strange city, but the creative imagination of the narrator. The red curtains, the engraving of the "Defeat of Reichenfels," and the crack in the marble of the dresser top animate his imagination: "The picture framed in varnished wood, the striped wall-paper, the fireplace with its mound of ashes, the table-desk with its lamp and opaque lampshade, and its glass ashtray, the heavy red curtains, the big sofa-bed upholstered with the same red velvety material, finally the dresser with its three drawers, the cracked marble, the brown package placed on it, and above it the picture, and the vertical lines of small gray insects extending to the ceiling." [1]

Similar descriptions return more and more frequently to the cracked marble top (that crevice for the imagination to slip into) which is directly under the picture hanging on the wall. The picture—a cabaret scene representing the owner, patrons, three soldiers sitting at a table, the boy holding the shoe-box—has no visible entrance. The narrator informs us that "this entrance door can only be situated on the absent wall of the drawing" (p. 48), that is, through the fourth dimension of our imagination. The crack in the marble top is the objective correlative for man's tendency to anthropomorphize things. Except that instead of describing its pathology, as he did in *Le Voyeur* and *La Jalousie*, Robbe-Grillet uses it to elaborate the imaginative processes. What he seems to be saying is that dream, day-dream, fantasy, imagination, the creative process are all related; that the factor which differentiates dream from imaginative creation or fiction is a matter of volition, direction, or perhaps even coherent organization. Mathias' day-dreaming foreshadows and reproduces his crime. The jealous husband's imagination re-creates what might have happened in the hotel room occupied by his wife and Franck. The doctor-narrator's imagination recreates the fiction of the events which may have preceded the soldier's death. The narrator's dream continues the story begun by his conscious imagination. After this the reader is almost never certain whether he is reading about the narrator's dream or the narrator's

imaginative re-creation of reality in terms of fictional possibilities. And so, the distinction between fiction and
reality breaks down. Perhaps I should say fiction becomes
reality: Mathias' day-dream is realized in the same way
that the husband's imagination is his reality seen through
the eyes of jealousy.

As the doctor either falls asleep or tries to reconstruct
what might have happened between the soldier and the
boy in the snowbound city, the frozen figures in the
picture come alive, begin to move and talk, the distinction between narrator and the tired sleepy soldier, sitting
at the table in the cabaret, breaks down, and the nightmare begins. "Are you asleep?" (p. 30), asks the boy. This
is not only a question directed at the soldier but also
Robbe-Grillet's narrative device of infrequent dialogue
which, by its very infrequency, gives the sentence which
is pronounced that "solid, monstrous, definitive *presence.*" [2] It is the beginning of the dream and the fusion of
dream-reality which the reader must participate in in
order to understand the qualitative dimension of the
book. This explains the hypnotic effect on A of X's words
in *Marienbad*. The rarity of spoken words in Robbe-
Grillet's novels gives them unusual weight and meaning.
Thus the questions and answers of the boy are significantly
charged yet also ambiguous: "What are you waiting for?"
or "What is in your package?" and the soldier's most
frequently repeated answer of "I don't know" or the boy's
"Why were you going to throw the box away?" or the
soldier will ask the boy if he has something to tell him
and the boy will answer "yes," but not say what.

Dans le labyrinthe is the most complex of Robbe-
Grillet's novels due to the ambiguity of the point of view
which shifts from the first person narrative "I" to the
third person narrative of the soldier's nightmare, then
back to the first person. Determining the narrator within
this novel is essential for its explication but doing so is, at
first, difficult because the novel seems to be about the endless peregrinations through the streets of a strange city of a
tired and fever-wracked soldier. This nameless soldier

whose friend has been killed at the front has been en-
trusted with that friend's few possessions (letters from his
fiancée, a bayonet, a watch, and a ring, all contained in an
oblong box—like a shoebox) which he is supposed to
deliver in person to the father (presumably the girl's but
this is not clear). The soldier has forgotten the name of
the recipient (it is not Martin, the dead soldier's name),
the name of the street, and the hour of the rendezvous.
Consequently he wanders from street-corner to street-
corner hoping to find or to be recognized by the unknown
man he is to meet. A young boy leads him to an inn, later
to his apartment, and then to a barracks for wounded
military personnel. The next day, as he is wandering
through the city, he is shot by two enemy soldiers who
are patrolling the streets on a motorcycle. A pedestrian,
who is a doctor, helps to carry him to an apartment, where
he dies. The narrative, in spite of this prosaic and chronological enumeration, is a hallucinated record of a night-
marish reality.

The novel begins with "I" and ends with "me" even
though the entire work appears to be written in the traditional third person. Robbe-Grillet suggests, however, that
on page 211 the first person possessive adjective "my" is
not to be overlooked.[3] The words, "On *my* [italics mine]
last visit, the third injection was useless," as Hazel Barnes
points out,[4] establish the doctor as the narrator of the
story. Bruno Hahn insists, and somewhat petulantly, that
Robbe-Grillet is the creator of this fiction.[5] We readily
grant that the author is always behind the personages of
his novels but why, we must ask, is the narrator a doctor?

If Sartre and Camus are Robbe-Grillet's spiritual fathers,
then perhaps we are not surprised to find a descendant of
Dr. Rieux (in *The Plague*), that modern incarnation of
Sisyphus, ministering to mankind in his endless struggle
against "la peste"—evil in any or all of its manifestations.
The "uselessness" of the third injection is, therefore, not
an insignificant detail. For, if the soldier is the analogue
for a sick humanity, then indeed it will take more than an
injection to cure him. This identification of the doctor

as narrator occurs, as Hazel Barnes points out, at almost the same distance from the end of the book as in *The Plague*. Camus writes: "It is time for the doctor, Bernard Rieux, to confess that he is the author." It is not irrelevant, as Bruno Hahn insists it is, that this doctor is the narrator. It is this very doctor, the prototype of "l'homme engagé," who, in the solitude of his own room, will recreate the fiction which is this novel. And in so doing, this doctor-artist (Robbe-Grillet himself) will minister to man's metaphysical ills.

If this city without name is yet another analogue for the human condition—as were Oran (*The Plague*), Amsterdam (*The Fall*), Kafka's village (*The Castle*), Dublin (*Ulysses*), or Bleston in Butor's *Emploi du temps*, then this meaningless journey through the labyrinth of a strange town by a sick soldier in quest of a father who cannot be found must surely be interpreted as the latest allegory of man's fate in an "absurd" world. The contents of the box then, though perhaps "meaningless," represent as Yvonne Guers states, the past heritage of man in capsule form.[6] I would not necessarily say, however, as she does, that the letters are "literature." How do we know? Letters are a means of communication, as is literature. We would have to give these letters a more generalized symbolic meaning, that is, as communication in any form. The bayonet with the cross-piece could, logically enough, be interpreted as a war symbol, but also as a religious one since the narrator dwells repeatedly on its resemblance to a cross. Time, as perhaps symbolized by the watch, is another heritage of man's, from which he cannot escape, and which is no doubt his most intimate possession. Yvonne Guers seems to think that the ring symbolizes riches, but why not marriage? Is not marriage a more significant social phenomenon than wealth in that marriage is man's institutionalized method for continuing the species?

These "trifling" objects have a far greater significance than their cursory treatment in the novel would seem to imply. They apparently stand for all the activities of man (past and present) as an individual, biological, social, religious, and political animal. It is not unimportant, it seems to me, that the man who is transmitting these "sacred" relics does so in vain and, in his attempt, dies a premature and violent death. Is not Robbe-Grillet commenting obliquely on the absence of teleological purpose? If the would-be father recipient of the dead soldier's possessions never appears, then the sick soldier's search for him resembles Estragon's and Vladimir's "waiting for Godot." They do not know who he is, nor when or even if he will come. If searching for the father and "waiting for Godot" are futile tasks, as the two authors seem to suggest, then these works are an artistic representation of the existential premise (Sartre's) that God does not exist. Furthermore, the setting for Robbe-Grillet's fiction is the "Defeat of Reichenfels," a defeat which may equally well stand for other similar defeats and which, by extension, could correspond to Roquentin's famous pronouncement: "Everything living is born without reason, is prolonged through weakness, and dies by encounter." [7] From Vincent Berger in Malraux' *Les Noyers de L'Altenburg*, who says he does not know why he was born or why he is alive or why he must die, to Meursault's alienation, and "strangeness," this is one of the dominant themes of modern existentialist literature.

Dans le labyrinthe communicates primarily man's contingency, his "délaissement," his solitude and alienation, and his "sickness unto death." As in *Ulysses*, *The Castle*, *L'Emploi du temps*, and *Les Gommes*, man's endless peregrinations through the city, which is a maze, suggest a search for self. If the soldier's search is futile and if he dies in the process, it is, no doubt, because he is transmitting a heritage which is found wanting and which accounts for the "Defeat of Reichenfels." " 'It's all over, you know, for now,' says the soldier. 'The war has ended . . .' Once more he feels his overwhelming fatigue" (p. 45). If this is so, if man's heritage has not prevented war and the death of man, then perhaps we should discard the box in the gutter and begin anew. Was not existentialism, which had such an immediate vogue at the end of World War II, an attempt to do just that? Was not Sartre's proclamation of no a priori morality his effort to annihilate custom and tradition in an attempt at a *table rase* from which to build a new morality? Was not the despair of existentialism the despair of a war-torn Europe whose vast culture and knowledge had still not prevented the atrocities of war? The whole concept of liberating man and then asking him to be "engagé" was, and still is, no doubt, the most significant step forward towards righting the imbalance of social and historical injustice.

Robbe-Grillet is not a moralist, but this novel is his strongest oblique statement to date in favor of "l'homme engagé." The philosophical orientation of the novel, however, depends on whether the soldier lives or dies. We are left with the impression that had the soldier realized the futility of his search and had he discarded the shoe-box of tradition, the three injections would have worked and he would have survived the bullet wound. But as Unamuno says, "man is a sick animal."

The soldier does indeed, at one point in the novel, contemplate throwing the box in the gutter, but he changes his mind when he sees the young boy watching him. Why does he change his mind? If the contents of the box do have symbolic value and if we were convinced that tradition was worthless, could we destroy our schools (communication), or our churches (religion), fire the military, or, as the Dadaists proclaimed, burn all the museums? Do we not perpetuate tradition for the sake of our youth and do we not feel the eyes of the young upon us? It is our adult sense of responsibility, no doubt, which inhibits such radical action. Such action is inconceivable unless the majority of the population agreed with Henry Miller that everything we are taught is false, that, as Miller phrases it, this is indeed "the time of the assassins." Few people feel as intensely as Miller does the cancerous nature of our modern civilized world. He would discard the double standard of those who preach one set of values to youth but, as adults, practice another. And so, in *Dans le*

labyrinthe, the soldier, out of habit and because he is
"sick" cannot discard the box. He dies. How can the
novelist change a society in which men are sick and in
which they are the creatures of habit? Robbe-Grillet's
work suggests that man must learn to resee the world.
Changing man's habit patterns, however, would depend
on altering his bad habits of perception. Until such change
occurs man will always be the victim rather than the
master of his environment. Man must reject "tragedy,"
accept "distance," and refuse to anthropomorphize the
world. He must learn to see the world with new eyes and
be capable of distinguishing between the world of objects
(inanimate and therefore geometric and linear) and the
world of man (animate and therefore complex and dis-
turbing). The equation "nouveau roman—homme nouveau" is the means by which he hopes to reeducate man.
Hence his insistence on the visual. Man must relearn to
see the world and, by implication, understand his own
relationship to it.

   With Sartre's work and to a lesser degree with Camus'
the reader is immediately aware of the moral and philosophical intent of the author's position. Robbe-Grillet
has been criticized for his undue preoccupation with technique—for the absence of content in his novels.[8] But since
the form of his novels is its content, Robbe-Grillet emerges
as an oblique moralist who is trying, within the context
of *Labyrinthe* to give his reader an historical as well as a
personal self-consciousness.

   ii

   The doctor-narrator's animation of the "Defeat
of Reichenfels" is comparable to Flaubert's animation of
Bruegel's *Temptation of St. Anthony.* The picture is the
point of departure for the novel. Butor uses a similar
technique in *L'Emploi du temps* in which the stained
glass window of the cathedral (Cain killing his brother
Abel) corresponds symbolically to the destructive power
of the city of Bleston. Similarly, the legend of Theseus
and the Minotaur, reproduced on the tapestries in the

museum of Bleston, stands for Jacques Revel's own attempts to solve the alienation from self experienced in the
large modern city.

The "new novelist's" use of pictures, tapestries, or
stained glass windows, though employed with skill and
originality, is not new. Maupassant, in *Une Vie*, uses a
tapestry representing the legendary misfortunes of
Pyramus and Thysbe as an ironic correlative for Jeanne's
life. The irony stems from the fact that she is unaware that
the events of her existence are already prefigured in em-
bryonic form on the tapestry. That instead of the tragic
fidelity in love and in death of the true legend, her
(Jeanne's) husband's infidelity and ubiquitous sex drive
(like that of the big rabbit which dwarfs the lion on the
tapestry) will not "kill" Jeanne but will wear her down to
an early senility. Irony depends on the reader's perception
of a reality hidden to the protagonist. Such reader insight
depends on some kind of author analysis (either through
dialogue or through direct interference in the narrative)
or, as Maupassant and Flaubert manage it, by objectify-
ing certain discrepancies. Thus Emma can be oblivious of
the fact that in the ecstasy of her happiness she is making
love on an old rotten bench. The astute reader, however,
perceives the irony of the juxtaposition and attributes this
"black humor" to Flaubert's point of view. Robbe-
Grillet rarely allows himself such intrusions because he,
no doubt, feels they destroy the "scientific" objectivity of
his novels by introducing a bias not related to his purpose.

In the elaboration of his fiction and in the absence of
irony Robbe-Grillet uses two related but distinct processes.
The imagination of his characters animates the material
environment until they fall victim to "tragic complicity,"
while at the same time the author (and hopefully the
reader) is aware of this tendency to anthropomorphize
nature and will, therefore, not be its victim. Robbe-
Grillet creates a distinction between the artist's conscious
manipulation of the "contamination" of things by man,
and man's unconscious enslavement by them. There will
be two value systems operating in Robbe-Grillet's work:

the unconscious animation of nature is called "tragic," while the artist's use of this fault (in man) for the elaboration of his art will be "creative." This explains, I believe, the curious interdependence in Robbe-Grillet's work between postcards, pictures, emotionally charged still-lives, and the subsequent animation of these still-lives within the work of art. There is a multiplicity of such picture-images in *Les Gommes*. The movie posters in *Le Voyeur* correspond thematically to the progression of the novel. The picture of the formal gardens in *Marienbad* will be the setting for much of the action which X and A will animate. Just as the Graal engraving in Julien Gracq's *Au château d'Argol* reinforces the theme of the novel, so the engraving of "Reichenfels" contains within it the seed for this novel. The excerpt from *Dans le labyrinthe* published in the September 1959 issue of the *NRF* is entitled "The Defeat of Reichenfels," a heading which, I believe, reinforces the hypothesis that the engraving on the wall, bearing the same name, explains the work.

Significant also is the fact that only man can order, relate, and give objects, images, and events any kind of meaning. This ordering of events, however, is a dimension of consciousness which, with the exception of the author and of X in *Marienbad*, is not an attribute of Robbe-Grillet's heroes. They are the victims of the very things which they, as men, should be capable of ordering and directing but do not. The title of the short pieces published recently as *Instantanés* (*Snapshots*, 1962) is revealing, for these photographs are not inanimate as one would expect, but replete with motion, texture, color, and continuity in time. These are "snapshots" of the psyche's affective life which starts and stops and moves— governed by the dictates of its own inner needs. An emotionally charged experience will be remembered statically as specific configurations of faces or things. But the meaning of such events is elusive. Associations of the mind imply motion in time and space. The real is, therefore, as the blurb on *L'Observatoire de Cannes* says, composed neither of the external world nor of pure fantasy

but is the result of the confluence of one and the other.
Robbe-Grillet's and Ricardou's descriptions are an attempt to recreate (there is no meaning without a perceiver) the surreality of the mind's life at every instant.

The doctor-narrator who freely creates a present and
hints at a future drawn out of the past affirms, like
Bergson, that duration is something other than history or
a system of laws. *Dans le labyrinthe* suggests that duration is *free* creation—that is, the creation of the *possible*.
The death of the soldier while demonstrating the tragedy
of a cause-and-effect determinism, also hints at the negation of such an inevitability. The narrator's creative
imagination gives us the feeling, as does Jean Ricardou's
book *L'Observatoire de Cannes,* that any moment can
be realized as a new moment, and that time can always
be freely created from the present towards the future. This
is the concept of "continuous creation" which Georges
Poulet considers an inherent part of twentieth-century
thought: not in the sense of creation by an omniscient
God but in the sense of creation by the mind of man.[9]
But creativity is related to choice. If man is free, and this
existential premise is right, then the creative imagination
is theoretically capable of curing or liberating man from
his "sickness." Robbe-Grillet's art demonstrates the pathology as well as the free possibilities of thought. Mathias
is enslaved by his imagination whereas the doctor-
narrator is the master of it. Robbe-Grillet's novels are
primarily demonstrations of enslavement.

The manner in which Robbe-Grillet alternates passages
in *Instantanés* between purely objective descriptions and
subjective involvement reinforces, in addition to the creative possibilities, his basic theme of the fundamental
separation between man and things. This dualism gives
Robbe-Grillet ample room for experimentation between
two equally defined artistic tendencies of his: the inherent
"romanticism" of his protagonist's imagination and Robbe-
Grillet's (the creative mind's) own imposition of order
and style. In "La Chambre secrète" (the last piece of
Instantanés) the visual description reminds us of the

exotic decor and flamboyant color of Delacroix' paint-
ings. The dedication to Gustave Moreau and the way in
which another verbal still-life painting is animated for the
sake of demonstrating the mind's (in this case the artist's)
play on imaginative possibilities reinforces this duality.
Like Moreau, Robbe-Grillet's imagination is capable of
the wildest flights, yet they both stop short of excess. In
each instance their romanticism is put to the service of a
disciplined, unsentimental conception. They both use a
strange combination of fantasy and realism, though
Moreau tended to imbue his objects with an inherent
symbolism which, of course, Robbe-Grillet does not do.
They both share a taste for elaborate detail which in
Moreau's *Salomé*, though within a grandiose tectonic
scheme, always remains carefully balanced.

The multiplicity of still-shots in Robbe-Grillet's latest
film script *L'Immortelle* reinforces his preoccupation with
the inanimate as it contrasts with the animate. We conclude, once again, that his emphasis on still-lives, like his
obsessive description of things, corresponds to visible projections of our affective life and to stimuli which govern
and affect its revolutions in time. (Simon's *Le Palace*
describes the continuous *revolution* in time of innumerable still-life possibilities). In each of Robbe-Grillet's
works the contrast between the animate and the inanimate
makes itself more strongly felt. Snapshots are things and
the artist's imagination which animates them is either
following the path of creative possibilities, as the constant
flickering of on-and-off lights in *Dans le labyrinthe* indicates, or, the soldier's imagination is subservient to these
things and therefore unable to extricate itself from the
labyrinth.

In Borges' story "The Garden of Forking Paths," Ts'ui
Pên says: "*I am withdrawing to write a book. And at another time: I am withdrawing to construct a labyrinth.*
Every one imagined two works: to no one did it occur
that the book and the maze were one and the same
thing." [10] Similarly in Robbe-Grillet's fiction it becomes
increasingly difficult to distinguish between art and

morality, between form and content, between dream and reality.

Borges, commenting on Schopenhauer and à propos of Art, remarks that "life and dreams are leaves of the same book: reading them in order is living; skimming through them is dreaming. In death we shall rediscover all the instants of our life and we shall freely combine them as in dreams." [11] It is the doctor-narrator's fictional and imaginative dream which, emanating as it does from the convergence of the soldier's death and the picture on the wall of his room, plunges us into the surreality of an elastic time in a universal continuum. But unlike Beckett's Malone, the narrator does not struggle with a dwindling pencil stub in an attempt to assert the superiority of mind over the gradual wasting away of the body. Malone informs the reader soon enough, and with "what tedium," that he will create four fictions of the mind. The doctor-narrator also creates a fiction, but it is indistinguishable from the soldier's nightmare.

Levin says that Joyce wanted to escape from the nightmare of history.[12] Joyce and Robbe-Grillet have, I believe, both written a book following Hawthorne's dictum: that of transcribing a dream with all its strange and gratuitous inconsistencies and metamorphoses, but at the same time writing a dream woven around a central idea. Finnegans Wake then is a dream focused on the totality of human experience as an absolute simultaneity of time and space. Earwicker's subconscious, like the soldier's nightmare, is the historical consciousness of the human race. Words are the raw materials of Earwicker's dream and Joyce relies, of course, on the etymology of the word as the prime substance of being and meaning. He deforms language, he condenses it, telescopes words, forms neologisms, and eliminates punctuation. Robbe-Grillet relies on a more traditional use of language reminiscent of The Dubliners. It is the composite structure or image which is significant rather than the humor of a neologism or the ambivalent interplay of two words, such as William and Richard to form "Rilchiam." Through the use of such contractions Joyce will be able to tell two or more simultaneous stories. Thus, one of the most famous passages of *Finnegans Wake*, "The Mookse and the Gripes," superimposes the "Mock-turtle and the Gryphon," on the "Fox and the Grapes." The difficulty and ambiguity of *Finnegans Wake* means that every reader, as he tries to decipher the meaning of the text, will give it a coherence dependent on his knowledge and experience. It is not a dream as much as it is an instrument for the fabrication of dreams.

Finnegans Wake, as Butor observes in his Introduction to the French translation,[13] becomes an intimate portrait of the reader since it is the reader's conscious or subconscious choice which he imposes on the meaning (never always clear) of neologisms, contractions, etc. This book is therefore a portrait of Everyman as H. C. E.'s (Here comes Everybody) initials indicate. Robbe-Grillet imposes a comparable subjectivity on his reader by forcing him to re-create the meaning and relationships of things and events within the structure of his novels. Since objects are merely "there," before they have any significance, it is the reader as dreamer, or the doctor-narrator as dreamer who will give the "chaos" of the juxtaposition some kind of meaning and order. *Finnegans Wake* and *Dans le labyrinthe* are, therefore, extremely intimate books, since it is a "portrait of myself" that I read into them. This is a further elaboration of the subjectivity of *Le Voyeur* since there the subjectivity is that of the protagonist Mathias. But the subjectivity of the doctor-narrator is potentially my own and I, as a reader, if my sense of historical consciousness is working, will be able to identify with the narrative more fully than was possible for *Le Voyeur*.

If tragic complicity is responsible for the nightmare of history, then the controlling metaphor is a labyrinth in which we all wander, perpetually lost in a place so strange and desolate that it cannot be properly conveyed by any of the modes of realism. To fully capture its meaning we must abandon ourselves to the dream and the nightmare whose inscrutable motives are, in "reality," incredibly reasonable. Metaphysics then becomes a branch of fantastic literature as it is in Poe whose dream ends in death but not in total extinction. For Poe the consciousness of the dreamer survives the death of the dream and becomes a witness to its disappearance. He describes this posthumous consciousness in the *Colloquy of Monos and Una* where, in experiencing the death of all his thoughts, the dead-alive person attains to the pure perception of a time without thought: "Let me term it a mental pendulous pulsation. It was the moral embodiment of man's abstract idea of Time . . . existing independently of any succession of events." [14]

Imaginary duration is therefore that of dream. Dream which exists within itself, possessing neither past nor future, functions in a perpetual present. In Robbe-Grillet's labyrinth it is not the consciousness of the soldier which survives (as it would in Poe) but the consciousness of the doctor-narrator. Conversely, the narrator's dream is the dead soldier's consciousness. Although this dream functions in the present, time (which is elastic) is a mode of human consciousness and corresponds therefore to the various stages of wakefulness or sleep of the doctor-narrator. It is this alternating identification of three human beings: the two soldiers and the doctor-narrator (four, if we as readers participate in the process) over a span of two centuries which gives this novel its extension in time. Time, as in Proust, will therefore expand or contract, not as a function of involuntary memory, but in terms of a historical consciousness. This consciousness will focus repetitively on various archetypal symbols such as the circle, the cross, or the mendalla: "under the heel, the imprinted depression of a cross in the middle of a circle in relief—that is, as far as the shoe itself is concerned, a cross in relief in the middle of a circular depression hollowed out in the rubber (a second round hole, not nearly as deep, whose extremely small diameter, still marks, perhaps, the center of the cross" (*Dans le labyrinthe*, p. 51).

The *cross* motif, used repeatedly in the *Labyrinthe* as the cross-piece on a bayonet and as a wall-paper pattern, occurs frequently enough in Robbe-Grillet's other novels to suggest that he uses it consciously and at critical moments makes it representative, in the Jungian sense, of a profound psychic experience. The front legs of the dead frog in *Le Voyeur* form a cross which attracts Mathias' attention immediately after he has killed Jacqueline. The revelation at the dinner table in *La Jalousie* that his wife is corresponding secretly with Franck is associated with the minute cross-stitching on a button on Franck's shirt. The soldier in *Labyrinthe*, after scrutinizing the form of the cross in the circle, tries to open a door which refuses to yield and then follows streets that seem to lead nowhere. If drawing a mendalla occurs, as Jung says, at moments of significant experience, or if the perception of a mendalla is equally important, then this juxtaposition with the soldier's futile search must reinforce the symbolic meaning of the novel.

Descriptions of snow, dust, and footprints will give an additional eerie timelessness to the nightmare—will suggest a continuity beyond the irrevocable and cyclical relationships of life and death—will give us an extension of consciousness in time and space beyond the frontiers of our normal daily limitations into the realm of the fantastic which, by its very surreality, communicates a meaning we sometimes only vaguely apprehend and which only Art can reveal. As Yves Berger states: "Everything resembles everything else and nothing changes." [15] The reader, like the lost soldier, feels that it is always "the same houses, the same deserted streets, the same gray and white layers of snow, the same cold." Objects lead to other objects, street-lights to other street-lights, intersections to other intersections. As in Kafka's work we find roads that fork, doors that do not open, false windows, and corridors that lead nowhere except to other corridors. The feeling of strangeness and alienation is complete.

Robbe-Grillet and Kafka, though the form of their novels is different, want to resolve the problem of "strangeness," to bring man closer to himself, closer to other men, and closer to the kingdom of heaven. *Amerika* suggests that the problem is primarily a psychological one, while *Dans le labyrinthe* indicates that perhaps the dilemma is a historical one. The box motif, which is crucial, runs through both *Amerika* and *Dans le labyrinthe* and is treated as the objective dramatization of internal problems. Critics seem to agree that, in *Amerika*, the box represents Karl's strong dependence on his parents, and the contents of the box (besides clothes and money)—a stale Veronese salami and a photograph of his parents—are repeated thematically and symbolically throughout the novel. Karl finally outgrows his dependence on parental figures—the authority of his father and his Oedipal attraction for his mother—and is ready to be admitted into "The Nature Theater of Oklahoma."

Dans le labyrinthe does not have that strong a resolution but the ending is, nevertheless, suggestive. While the enemy is occupying the town and in the midst of a violent quarrel between the doctor and the fake cripple, the boy is sitting on the floor, his legs spread "forming a very open V" (p. 202). He is pressing the box tightly to his chest with his arms. The V theme (Victoire?) is repeated several times. There is, in addition to the repetitions, a photographic intensity in the description. The V position of the boy's legs contrasts with the folded legs of the boy in the engraving, thereby indicating two boys of two different centuries. There is therefore evolution in time from a cross-legged boy holding a box on his chest, to a V-legged boy also holding, not the same shoe-box, but a newer different one of tin. This constant emphasis of the V suggests a solution even though Robbe-Grillet does not develop one overtly. The problem, as in *Les Gommes*, is the reader's. The soldier's violent and premature death is comparable to Wallas' shooting his father. The reader who has solved the Oedipus complex in *Les Gommes* must now undertake the identical task of trying to find an answer which gives a plausible explanation to the soldier's death.

Once again, as the title *Dans le labyrinthe* suggests, a Greek theme intrudes into the novel. But Robbe-Grillet's

work is obviously not an exact copy of the Cretan labyrinth. He like Sartre, Giraudoux, Anouilh, and so many
others, has altered Greek legend to suit his purpose. According to the Greek version the Athenians, conquered
by Minos, king of Crete, were forced, every year, to send
a tribute of seven youths and seven maidens to be de-
voured in the labyrinth by the Minotaur. As everyone
knows, Theseus, with Ariadne's help, slew the Minotaur
and delivered Athens. Readers of *Dans le labyrinthe*,
however, are aware of the fact that no monster is killed.
But perhaps the soldier who dies provides a clue, for in the
pocket of his overcoat is a big marble with a *black* center
(p. 142). According to the Greek myth lots were cast for
those unfortunates who were to embark for Crete in the
black ship. Those youths and maidens who drew black
balls instead of white ones were to be eaten by the
Minotaur. Robbe-Grillet informs us that the soldier has
acquired the marble at the barracks (p. 143) where, because his coat is wet, he is given the dry one of another
soldier (probably dead). It is in the pocket of this coat
that he finds the marble with the *black* center.

Now, if this marble is Robbe-Grillet's equivalent for the
"black ball," which the soldier acquires by "chance" (his
military destiny by virtue of birth in time and place), and
he, as the title and contents of the book so strongly imply,
is "in the labyrinth," then he is one of those unfortunate
youths whose draft board has chosen as flesh for the
Minotaur. The modern equivalent of the ancient monster
can only be the war machine since the soldier is killed in
the streets by the enemy. The novel therefore seems to
imply that modern man is not only sick, but doomed to
extinction unless a young Theseus, capable of eliminating the "monster," leads the way out of the labyrinth.

The reader must keep in mind and combine two factors
I have already referred to: first of all, that for Robbe-
Grillet content is a function of form and secondly, apply
the symbolic nature of the box's contents to the equally
symbolic allusion of the boy holding the box. If the sick
soldier stands for a sick humanity, if the box's contents

symbolize man's racial, social, individual, and political inheritance, and if a young boy whose legs form the image of a prominent V is a symbol of youth, that is, of a future humanity, then the image of a young Theseus clutching the box to his chest, while not saying so overtly, does nevertheless state covertly that there is a way out of the labyrinth if youth, the future's collective Theseus, will only kill the Minotaur.

In conclusion, the novel recreates the thought processes of the doctor-narrator's mind which blends the hypothetical activities of people represented in a picture hanging on the wall entitled "The Defeat of Reichenfels" (identified as a print of the last century), with "real" events which the narrator "imagines" might have preceded the soldier's death. The soldier's death is the pretext for the doctor-narrator to re-create and fuse the fiction of two battles, one dating from the nineteenth century, one from the twentieth, into a story actually written by Robbe-Grillet and entitled *Dans le labyrinthe*. But the Greek motif, whose basis is the war between Athens and Crete, gives the "Battle of Reichenfels" a timeless dimension and the "Defeat of Reichenfels" is symbolic of everybody's defeat in war in the same sense that the soldier's death is symbolic of every soldier's death.

The picture on the wall is, therefore, both a statement of the problem and a solution to the problem. The publication of *Instantanés* illustrates, once again, the importance Robbe-Grillet attaches to the symbolic content of still-lives. Each still-life and each picture is the hidden voice of the author. Editorial Omniscience has been objectified. It is not heard—it is seen and the reader must translate the visible into audible meaning. Typical of this new art form is the fact that the reader has been shown and not told. If we are to understand Robbe-Grillet's work (this is "l'école du regard") we must conceptualize what we see. Robbe-Grillet's Art—his technique as well as his moral intent—is subservient to what is seen. The visible is, in turn, subordinate to his desire to demonstrate the fallacy of "tragic complicity." His novels as well as his film scripts evolve within this context.

"Tragic complicity" handled symbolically within this novel explains the death of the soldier. His death combined with the "Defeat of Reichenfels" give us the "picture" of the novel, the still-life of the doctor's affective life—the objectification of his imagination as daydreaming and as nightmare. The nightmare is the symbolic historical consciousness of Man— the "tragic complicity" of man's collective unconscious in terms of war. But the novel which recreates the nightmare of history and which dwells self-consciously (as it does) and creatively on hypothetical alternatives demonstrates the free play of imaginative possibility—the imaginative possibilities of a mind which refuses tragedy and is therefore free to give some kind of meaning and order to the chaos of innumerable alternatives. *Dans le labyrinthe*, like any novel, is the ordering of such innumerable alternatives. But the extreme self-consciousness of the organization reintroduces the authorial omniscience which so many modern novelists have been trying to suppress. This only means, I suppose, that inevitably certain novels, due to inherent structural characteristics, must rely on authorial interference particularly when, as with Robbe-Grillet, the author is demonstrating the difference between the pathology of "tragic complicity" and the imaginative *free* creation of the artist.

ONLY A FEW MONTHS before *Last Year at Marienbad* won the 1961 Golden Lion at the Venice Film Festival, distributors in France had decided that it was too difficult for the average moviegoer and had refused to show it. But they did show it after it won the award, and no sooner had it opened at the Studio Publicis on the Champs-Elysées than Alain Resnais' production of Robbe-Grillet's script was breaking all attendance records, even outdrawing such other favorites as Antonioni and Bergman. The Press, from the far left to the extreme right, devoted more space to this picture than to any other in recent memory and the opinions expressed represented every conceivable shade of critical divergence.

Unsympathetic critics wrote that it was a magnificent monument to boredom—"a swindle, a mockery of the public's intelligence." It was attacked as a picture absolutely lacking in human warmth—"an interminable procession of two icebergs before a rococo mirror," or a world peopled by robots dressed in evening jackets. Sympathetic critics saw it as a "passionate film," a marvelous love story, and the culmination of film art. Jean de Baroncelli wrote that *Marienbad* represented in moviemaking what Picasso's "Les Demoiselles d'Avignon" did in the history of painting. *Marienbad* was soon being hailed as the first cubist film. Critics spoke of it as the application of Einsteinian relativity to the cinema (a formula Roland Barthes had already used in describing *Les Gommes*) and as revolutionary as Schoenberg's twelve-tone scale.

The excitement was the result of a technical revolution in cinematography, since, here, at last, the authors had succeeded in filming space as a function of psychological time. Film critics, unfamiliar with Robbe-Grillet's scrambling of time in terms of memory, reality, or fantasy were confused, angered, and hostile. Their incomprehension was no different from the absence of insight of literary critics when Robbe-Grillet's novels were first published. For *Marienbad* is the filmed equivalent of all the innovations Robbe-Grillet had already imposed. In fact, the manner in which his novels are "seen" indicates a logical evolution of his art towards the "ciné-roman" (the "film-novel"). *Marienbad* is therefore as "real" and as "true" as are the inner optics of the mind's eye associating the images of experience or of reality in the past, the present, and the future. This movie has captured the inner dimensions of the psyche exteriorized as things. It has projected pure thought, pure dream, and pure inner life. Thus the fundamental conflict which George Bluestone (*Novels into Film*) sees between the novel and the film has broken down. These two art forms are not necessarily mutually exclusive.

Marienbad opens, like *Hiroshima mon amour*, with a sustained and elaborate introduction which, in *Hiroshima*, Resnais called the "opera." Penelope Houston calls the opening of *Marienbad* the "overture." [1] As the organ music begins to fade, a grave, impersonal, and very quiet voice is heard. The voice becomes stronger and clearer as the first images appear: long, empty corridors with baroque ceilings and mirrored walls. The voice continues in an incantatory manner as the eye or the camera moves slowly through carpeted, luxurious surroundings: "Once again I walk, once again, along these corridors, across these *salons*, these galleries, in this edifice from another century, this huge, luxurious, baroque hotel." The camera moves from a theater poster, a print of a formal garden, a row of numbered doors, through labyrinthine halls to a darkened *salon* where motionless and abstracted people sit watching the stage. The voice of an actor takes over from the unseen narrator and the actress next to the man on the stage says: "Voilà maintenant, je suis à vous." Curtain, lights, and a strong sense of identification of the movie audience with the theater audience on the screen. This identification is important for the impact of the film will depend on the viewer's ability to participate in the drama which will be enacted for him. The opening is hypnotic and the spectator is drawn into the film. The incantatory voice of the narrator, the maze of corridors, the play within the play set the stage through sound and movement for optimal empathy between the movie audience and the film.

There is a significant identification which seems to take place between the audience and the hero or the heroine on the screen. One of the reasons for the extreme popularity of the movies is the fact that this projection between viewer and film image does occur so that, for the duration of the movie, the spectator may become a personage of strength, beauty, or achievement. For a period of ninety minutes he is able to identify with the prowess and conquests (love, action, etc.) of the actors who are performing on the screen. The realism of a movie, says Robbe-Grillet, "draws us towards it out of our lethargy with a violence which we would search for in vain in a corresponding written text, be it a novel or a script." [2]

A novel of Balzac or the work of Proust, if we are to believe the new dogma, is no longer as involving as it once was. By analogy then, a movie which is anecdotal or which tells a story will be equally unsatisfying, for if the new reader or the new spectator is as exigent as Robbe-Grillet, Sarraute, Resnais, and many others claim he is, then the traditional narrative modes are no longer capable of satisfying his demands. With Sarraute's work the reader must necessarily concentrate all his attention if he is to understand her art and resolve the narrative difficulties. Robbe-Grillet claims the attention of the reader by giving his work a detective aura and by creating a puzzle whose meaning must be solved if it is to be understood. The reader must therefore recreate the work of art himself and in doing so he participates more actively than ever before in the actual narrative process. The dislocation of time, though an integral part of Robbe-Grillet's art, means, in part, that if he is to understand the function of the protagonist's "imaginations," the reader must reconstruct some kind of linear chronology in terms of past and present.

In *Marienbad*, Robbe-Grillet's juxtaposition of past, present, and future in terms of memory, reality at hand, and fantasy, without regard for chronology but only in terms of the mind's inner necessity, as it associates objects of a particular sequence, includes in the creative process, as Eisenstein insists it should, the emotions and mind of the spectator:

> The spectator is compelled to proceed along that selfsame creative road that the author traveled in creating the image. The spectator not only sees the represented elements of the finished work, but also experiences the dynamic process of the emergence and assembly of the image just as it was experienced by the author. And this is, obviously, the highest possible degree of approximation to transmitting visually the author's perception and intention in all their fullness, to transmitting them with "that strength of physical palpability" with which they arose before the author in his creative work and his creative vision.[3]

Eisenstein points out that the strength of "montage" resides in the fact that the spectator is drawn into a creative act in which his individuality is not subordinated to the author's individuality but is fused with the author's intention in a manner not unlike the fusion that takes place between the individuality of a great actor and a great playwright in the creation of a classic scenic image:

> In fact, every spectator, in correspondence with his individuality, and in his own way and out of his own experience— out of the womb of his fantasy, out of the warp and weft of his associations, all conditioned by the premises of his character, habits and social appurtenances, creates an image in accordance with the representational guidance suggested by the author, leading him to understanding and experience of the author's theme.[4]

The theme of *Marienbad* is a "persuasion." It is a persuasion, however, only if the spectator follows the intricate maze of images as they record A's progression from initial indifference towards X all the way to her final submission to him.

The action takes place in what Robbe-Grillet (in the preface to his script) describes as "a grand hotel, a sort of international palace, immense, baroque, with a décor at once sumptuous and icy: a universe of columns, marble, gilded panels, statues, servants in rigid stances; a clientele rich, polished, anonymous, unemployed. Seriously but without passion they play society's inevitable games—cards, dancing, vacant conversations, pistol-shooting. Inside this closed and stifling world, people and things alike seem caught in an enchantment." Among the enchanted inhabitants of the château are a beautiful young woman (played by Delphine Seyrig), a man (played by Sacha Pitöeff) who is "perhaps her husband," and the stranger X (Giorgio Albertazzi) who follows her relentlessly and persuades her finally to leave with him. The narrator, X, insists and finally convinces A that they did meet "last year at Marienbad." This is a conviction which gradually spreads and acquires independent form on the screen so that what the audience sees is the progression of the imagery of this persuasion.

So far there has been no discrepancy between the film and the script. If a discrepancy does exist (as I believe it does) it will depend on the nature of this persuasion and the answer to the question which the spectator and A must be asking themselves: did X and A meet "last year at Marienbad?" In answer to this question Resnais has said that he would not have shot the film unless X and A had met, whereas, Robbe-Grillet has insisted that the couple did not meet the year before: "This movie is no more than the story of a persuasion, and one must remember that the man is not telling the truth." [5] The movie itself, as Resnais shot it, is sufficiently ambiguous to allow for either interpretation. The script, however, is not, and the entire meaning of the persuasion depends on the fact that

X and A did not meet the year before. We have therefore not one work of art but two different ones for, as George Bluestone says, "the filmist becomes not a translator for an established author, but a new author in his own right." [6] The meaning of this film is almost diametrically opposed to the meaning of Robbe-Grillet's script. What comes through most forcefully in the film is a sense of A's final liberation. This coincides not only with Resnais' idea that the two had met the year before but with his interpretation of the script and consequently its filming. For Resnais, A is a young woman imprisoned among the bored guests of a luxurious hotel. She is like a fairy princess caught in an enchanted castle. The young man X rescues her and leads her to something unknown in an alive outside world.[7] The final lines of the script, however, negate this liberation and Resnais, to be consistent, should have left them out. These lines are a capsule summary of Robbe-Grillet's philosophic purpose.

Marienbad, like his previous novels, is a demonstration, an example of what can happen to those who humanize the world about them. A is another victim of "tragic complicity" and what we witness is a breakdown in the "neutrality" of her environment. At the end X comments on the fact that it seemed at first impossible to lose oneself among the statues, the alleys, and the geometric shapes of the formal gardens. The final lines state that A is in the process of losing herself forever, alone with X. There is no mention of liberation. They are not even together for she is "alone." This is indeed a sombre finale to the "they lived happily ever after" prince-princess fairy tale stereotype. Resnais' picture, though technically fascinating, is nothing more than the traditional love triangle. Within the context of *his* vision therefore he plays down A's evolving alienation and "complicity" with things. But Robbe-Grillet's script is a theorem and his demonstration depends entirely on A's inability to distinguish between dream and reality. Her anxiety, gradually building up to a psychotic fear, has been toned down in the movie.

Curiously enough Robbe-Grillet has leaned over back-

wards to stress the identity of vision and the harmony of
his collaboration with Resnais. Yet Robbe-Grillet would
have preferred more "spectacular" shots of A's hysterical
scenes.[8] He insists that the changes Resnais made in the
script reinforced his (Robbe-Grillet's) original intention
and vision. The collaboration was so close, says Robbe-
Grillet, that the two of them were to sign the final version
thus indicating an absolute co-authorship. But they have
not signed it together, and Robbe-Grillet, for reasons of
"honesty" as he phrases it, has published the original
script as it was before the shooting of the film. Why? Why
did they not sign it together and why does not the published version of the "ciné-roman" coincide with the revi-
sions if they were, as Robbe-Grillet claims, always in the
line of his own original intention? The answer depends,
once again, on the fact that Resnais has changed the
original meaning of the film and Robbe-Grillet has preferred to keep the first version because it suits his artistic
purposes better. *Marienbad*, as he wrote it, evolves directly
from the metaphysical content of his novels. Moreover,
in their initial interviews, Resnais had agreed to film
three more of Robbe-Grillet's plots and at least two of his
novels. Robbe-Grillet, however, with *L'Immortelle*, is now
filming his own plots.[9] This is perfectly logical, for the
author of a script, if he is to see it filmed unaltered, should
direct it himself. In fact, the most desirable relationship
is one in which the author of a script also directs the movie
he is acting in. Molière's activities as playwright and actor,
Orson Wells' *Citizen Kane*, and his many film adapta-
tions reveal advantages to be derived from an absolutely
unified work of art.

Robbe-Grillet has written novels and a script which
need not be distorted in order to be filmed. His decision
to assume control of the total process is a logical one
and we can now look forward to movies which will be an
extension of his aesthetic and philosophic theories in
which, as in his novels, the form will be its content. This
is true of *Marienbad* in spite of the change in emphasis.
It is precisely because Resnais emphasized certain gestures

and made A's fear less dramatic that the content of the film has changed. That is why X's last words in the film are, I feel, out of context with Resnais' production. They can only mean that the persuasion has worked and that A is in effect a new prisoner of the things she has anthropomorphized and which are the catalysts (as things were catalysts for Mathias) responsible for fusing reality and fantasy. Her love for X, if that is what we must call her departure with him, has the same compulsive neurotic aura about it as the behavior of Mathias and the jealous husband.

What has usually happened in the past during the mutation from novel into film has not been a conversion but a paraphrase.[10] George Bluestone refers to the inevitable disappointment novelists must accept when their novels are adapted into film. For the director, at least in the past, could not transfer the language of the novel onto the screen. All he could do was use characters and incidents which, like some mythic legend, have detached themselves from style and become autonomous. It is these autonomous entities which are filmed. That is why, says Bluestone, there is no necessary correspondence between the excellence of a novel and the quality of a film based on it.[11]

Robbe-Grillet's novelistic technique has rendered such a paraphrase unnecessary. Whereas the traditional novel renders the illusion of space by going from point to point in time, Robbe-Grillet's novels, like the film, render time by going from point to point in space—hence the detailed visual descriptions of things. Formerly, though the subject of the novel and a film might be the same, the content, that is language versus image, was different. The twentieth-century novel, that of Proust or Joyce, for example, has relied for its effect on the explosion of words, whereas Robbe-Grillet's novels again, like the film, rely for their effect on the explosion of visual images. Words in literature, as language, have always stood between the perceiver and the symbolized percepta, while Robbe-Grillet's objects, as things and images, come to us through word-images rather than word-ideas. The meaning of his novels passes through a minimal distortion of conceptual apprehension.[12]

The language of the novel seems to have relied most frequently on a symbolic medium that stands between the perceiver and what is perceived. The process of language as thought (the author's) has always interfered with the direct apprehension of things. Faulkner's elliptical, often oblique descriptions of phenomena were a step away from "literature." Hemingway's direct objective style is another example of the emancipation of the novel from the stream of consciousness. Sartre praised this "objective" technique in Dos Passos as the most effective way of rendering the subconscious visible.[13] Moreover, the earlier "objective" novels of Flaubert or Maupassant lend themselves more readily to film adaptation than the stream of consciousness novels of Proust or Joyce or Sarraute. This is indeed a point of aesthetic divergence. Sarraute insists that the novel, as hers do, should cultivate the terrain which the movies cannot. "The movies gather and perfect what the novel is abandoning," says Sarraute in L'Ere du soupçon, though perhaps, as Michel Mourlet insists, it should be phrased the other way around: "The novel gathers and perfects what the movies are abandoning." [14] But since the novel as a genre cannot be easily defined and since it must, as Henry James says, thrive on freedom, I would hesitate to restrict it in this manner. Le Voyeur and La Jalousie, though cinematic, remain beautiful novels. Their style, which is as close to the film in novel form as it is possible to get remains "novelistic." Nor are they scripts. This is evident the moment we compare them to the script for Marienbad.

While much of Marienbad reads like a novel we are nevertheless conscious of the filming directions for close-ups, travelling, etc. Such movement in a novel would naturally be inferred from the displacement of a particular personage. Thus, if La Jalousie were being filmed the camera would make a ninety degree turn from the contemplation of the banana grove in order to focus on A...

in her room combing her hair. But since the camera is nonselective in detail whereas A... combing her hair has specific meaning for the jealous husband, we would need a close-up in order to restrict the viewer's field of vision, in order to have it coincide with the *particular* selectivity of the husband. Every detail which the husband's attention focuses on and which reinforces his jealousy can be isolated in a close-up, thus restricting the spectator's field of vision and at least the visual quality of his perception. With the proper lighting, gestures, and angle of vision, the camera might be able to render the sensuous detail of A... combing her black hair which Robbe-Grillet infuses in his novel. Isolating the centipede, stains, A...'s fingers clutching a dinner knife or the folds of the table cloth, all of which are described visually in the novel, can be filmed in a close-up, juxtaposed with the proper editing, and given the same relationship on the screen which they have in the novel.

La Jalousie (with all due allowance for differences in chronology, psychological time, objective correlatives, and voice narrative) is not as different from Robert Montgomery's *Lady in the Lake* as Colette Audry or Bruce Morrissette imply.[15] Since everything is seen through the eyes of the jealous husband and since his jealousy only becomes meaningful as a result of the selection and juxtaposition of objects and events, the invisible eye of the camera would correspond to the invisible presence of the unseen husband who spies on his wife through the jalousies, through windows, through doors, and in his imagination. The few times that the husband is "en scène," his presence could be rendered, as in *The Lady in the Lake*, by a mirror reflection (preferably a back or shadow view) so that the identification between the viewer and the screen personage not be destroyed by too obvious and imposition of recognizable features. Robbe-Grillet's art is therefore not antipodal to Montgomery's as Colette Audry maintains. She is talking about a movie and a novel: two different art forms. If Robert Montgomery transforms his camera into a personage and if

Robbe-Grillet in his novel transforms the jealous husband into a camera we must, however, not forget the difference of genres.

What the reader does in *La Jalousie* is project the descriptions on the screen of his mind's eye—hence the critics' qualification of such writing as "l'école du regard." If the novel were filmed the descriptions of things and objects would be rendered spatially on celluloid. The director would have to find cinematic equivalents for recurring words like "vide" (empty) or "silence" or "violence" which are used frequently in Robbe-Grillet's novels to reinforce a mood. But this is not difficult to render pictorially. The emptiness of the plantation house, while A... is in town with Franck, can be filmed by making the camera move from one empty room to another and the husband's inner emptiness finds its correlative in the empty rooms through which he is walking. The mounting violence of Mathias' sexual drive will be filmed as waves slamming more and more violently against the jetty or the rocks. The camera will begin by filming little waves and then progressively bigger ones. The "silence" in *Marienbad* was achieved by travelling through empty corridors but also by two other devices: either the total absence of sound where sound should have been heard, thus suggesting a dreamlike quality, or the disproportionate loudness of running water or crunching gravel in other scenes. The selectivity of the camera and the soundtrack can thus control the emotional intensity of the film. The isolation of a detail will correspond to an object under immediate scrutiny, and of great oneiric significance, such as the centipede on the wall (or its stain) or the fragments of the broken glass in *Marienbad*. Thus, in *L'Immortelle*, we have close-ups of people alternating with distance shots in which the personages appear no larger than flies.

Within the context of *Marienbad* the use of broken glass and its juxtaposition and association with shoes, A's room, the heel breaking on the garden path have specific meaning for A (hence also for the viewer) who sees or

imagines these events. Symbolically the broken glass corresponds appropriately to the fact that A's grasp on reality
is breaking down, i.e., she begins to doubt her own memory
while at the same time fantasy images of rape, murder,
and suicide begin to intrude on her consciousness. Then
when the guard-rail in the garden crumbles, the theme of
things breaking is reinforced. Since what happens pictorially in the film corresponds so frequently to the inner
time-space dimensions of the characters' psyches we must
relate the thematic repetition of spatial events to their
unseen (but necessarily inferred) counterparts as the time
sequence of a personage's affective life. Since at the beginning of the film A rejects the possibility of their encounter
"last year" while, at the end of the story, she leaves with
X, because she now believes in such an encounter, it is
obvious that the "persuasion" has been effective. She does
not leave joyfully or happily however. In fact the persuasion has taken place at great cost for A: fear, anxiety,
dreams of violence. If leaving M and the decadence of the
château is a liberation, her personality breakdown is another enslavement. Whereas at first she was enslaved by
the habit and convention of card playing, theater going,
target practice, all objectified as the baroque decadence
of an old château, she now is enslaved by a different
phenomenological order and one wonders if the previous
enslavement is not preferable.

The fusion of reality and fantasy into visual images is
not only typical of dreams and the dream process but,
psychologists now tell us, plastic word-representation, as
it occurs in dreams, is related to the thought process and
alienation of the mentally ill. We say that someone is
insane when he can no longer distinguish between fantasy
and reality. All of us have, no doubt, experienced the immediacy of dream "reality" which is as real as our waking
hours until that moment of wakefulness when we can
pick up the threads of continuity where they left off the
night before and therefore isolate the dream as a phenomenon of sleep. If we assume that Mathias, the jealous
husband, and A in *Marienbad* are ill, in varying degrees,

then their thought processes, rendered as pictorial images, are psychologically justifiable—this, in addition to the fact that they are justifiable from the literary and cinematic points of view. The difficulties of transforming a novel into film are, it seems, not unlike the difficulties of the sleeping mind as it changes verbal reality into the distorted, often grotesque, symbolic images of dreams. Freud insists that this process is not always an easy one:

In order to get some idea of its difficulty, imagine that you had undertaken to replace a political leading article in a newspaper by a series of illustrations; you would have to abandon alphabetic characters in favour of hieroglyphics. The people and concrete objects mentioned in the article could be easily represented, perhaps even more satisfactorily, in pictorial form; but you would expect to meet with difficulties when you came to the portrayal of all the abstract words and all those parts of speech which indicate relations between the various thoughts, e.g., particles, conjunctions, and so forth. With the abstract words you would employ all manner of devices: for instance you would try to render the text of the article into other words, more unfamiliar perhaps, but made up of parts more concrete and therefore more capable of such representation. This will remind you of the fact that most abstract words were originally concrete, their original significance having faded; and therefore you will fall back on the original concrete meaning of these words wherever possible. So you will be glad that you can represent the "possessing" of an object as a literal, physical "sitting upon" it (posses—*potis* + *sedeo*). This is just how the dream-work proceeds. In such circumstances, you can hardly demand great accuracy of representation, neither will you quarrel with the dream-work for replacing an element which is difficult to reduce to pictorial form, such as the idea of breaking marriage vows, by some other kind of breaking, e.g., that of an arm or leg. In this way you will to some extent succeed in overcoming the awkwardness of rendering alphabetic characters into hieroglyphs.[16]

The content of dream-thoughts is represented in the dream as objects and activities. This is its raw material.

The dream therefore differs as much from our verbal thought processes as the movies and the novel differ from each other. This does not mean that one activity is necessarily better than the other of that one art form is superior to the other. When a dream or a movie must represent those parts of speech which indicate thought relations, e.g., "because," "therefore," "but," they must inevitably find a substitute method for rendering the transition or, as far as pictorial form is concerned, leave them untranslated. And so, the lack of transition in the fantasy images of Mathias, the jealous husband, or A in *Marienbad* corresponds to the kind of dream sequence Freud is referring to. Mathias' spells of dizziness and A's nightmares obviously depend for their elaboration on the description or the filming of related hieroglyphs.

Though Robbe-Grillet's novels are made up of objects, activities, sequential images and hieroglyphs it is the narrative style which, as always, presents the most difficulty. His novels are not scripts; yet compared to the work of Proust or Sarraute, they are easily adaptable. To translate *A la recherche du temps perdu* into film would be to limit it to its anecdotal material. Its essence would be lost. The novels of Nathalie Sarraute are not filmable. There are, therefore, varying degrees of adaptation as one art form is translated into another. Thus, the technicolor version of *Le Rouge et le noir* with Gerard Philippe and Danielle Darrieux (directed by Claude Autant-Lara) fails as a movie because it tries to reproduce Sorel's inner monologue which is not cinematic but literary. The audience-actor identification is broken every time the action stops to let Julien think audibly (but with closed lips) as the voice emanates from the screen. A movie can be realistic in the extreme or it may be a fantasy creation, but when it tries to be literary it fails simply because that is not its domain. The purpose of the film is to show, not to tell. Thus Harry, in Hemingway's *The Snows of Kilimanjaro* can tell the reader about the stinking breath of death crouching on his chest. The movie, however, if it is to be effective, must find a pictorial equivalent. The directors of this film with Gregory Peck as Harry have, I believe, successfully rendered a pictorial equivalent for death by introducing the presence of a native witch doctor. The delirious Harry and the viewers can now see the painted face of the witch doctor which the viewers, if they wish, may interpret as the very presence of "stinking death." This represents a successful "translation" of one incident even though the film itself is not outstanding.

But how can film give us the pictorial equivalent of Robbe-Grillet's geometric, "neutral," and "cleansed" descriptions? Simply filming these objects is not enough since, once projected on the screen, they assume the same realistic dimensions which the viewer attributes to them in real life. Registering objects on celluloid does not necessarily neutralize them for the perceiver; there is always a human eye to interpret them. How then can the film director translate the "distance" which a geometric description implies onto film? Perhaps the most effective way is to use the concept of "distance" literally and film objects from afar. The problem, as with the novel, is how to introduce authorial comment or judgment without obviously interrupting the narrative sequence. In the novel it is the optical adjective that measures, situates, limits, and defines an object in space which gives us this "distance." As the personage becomes emotionally involved in his environment these descriptions become more and more traditional in that Robbe-Grillet uses emotionally charged verbs, adverbs, and the equivalent of the anthropomorphic adjective: the objective correlative. In like manner, the lens of the camera can zoom in to isolate an object or it can maintain its "distance" (emphasized in *L'Immortelle*), the lighting can change, and it is even conceivable that variations of black and white, blending imperceptibly into color, might be introduced to correspond to various stages of emotional involvement.[17] Light intensity variations were used in *Marienbad* to indicate transitions from actual reality to fantasy.

No two people ever see the same movie or ever read

the same book. Our own experience in talking to friends about a particular film or about a novel by Flaubert or Zola should soon convince us that we see and read, not the author's work of art, but our own. In this sense Resnais is justified in making *Hiroshima mon amour* and *Marienbad* mean all things to all people. But in doing so he has soft-pedalled the humanitarian orientation which Duras gave her script as well as the particular theorem Robbe-Grillet was demonstrating in *Marienbad*. The logical conclusion to Eisenstein's montage sequence is what Resnais has done. But the danger of this conclusion is that, if the author refuses to give his work meaning, it *will* be meaningless. This is also the dilemma of non-objective art as practiced by those speed virtuosi who splash paint on canvas with frenzied rapidity. The configurations of paint may be interesting but they remain just what they are: splashes of paint in spite of the sensuous quality of "texture." "Splashed accidents" may be aesthetically pleasing but do they have meaning? Unless a nonobjective painter like Kandinsky, or Klee, or Nicholas de Staël deliberately juxtaposes colors to achieve a desired result, unless the transitions of color interact or give movement or create a harmonic fantasy akin to music, the poetry of color is no more meaningful and just as ephemeral as our day-dreams engendered by the contemplation of cloud formations. Contemplating cloud formations may be fun but is it art, that is, is either the cloud or the process of contemplating it art? If art depends on active yet controlled imaginative processes then Robbe-Grillet's novels are not meaningless nor are they merely an exhibition of technique as many critics affirm.[18] Resnais' production of *Marienbad* unfortunately tends to reinforce the notion of a technique virtuoso whereas, in fact, Robbe-Grillet's "message," concealed as it is in the form of his work, is as meaningful and significant and far more exciting artistically, than, for instance, "Les Chemins de la liberté." I cite Sartre deliberately to suggest the degree of Robbe-Grillet's commitment. No critic, if he understood Robbe-Grillet, could say that he is uncommitted.

Like Camus or Gide or Proust he is primarily an artist and for the true artist content *is* a function of form.

How did his particular form evolve? In addition to the influences of the movies we should add the impact of the American novel of Dos Passos, Faulkner, Hemingway, Steinbeck, and Caldwell which, after 1920, due to good translations by Coindreau, Raimbault, and others, began to exert an influence on French letters. In an article in the August 1946 issue of *The Atlantic Monthly*, Sartre says that Hemingway taught French writers who were tired of their own tradition of psychological analysis how to depict without commentaries, without explanations, without moral judgments, the actions of their characters; that Dos Passos revealed the falsity of the unity of action and that his "objective" technique depicting the workings of the human subconscious produced a technical revolution among French writers; that Faulkner's dislocation of time was an important artistic discovery.[19]

Another significant innovation of the American novel was its focus on bums, half-wits, idiots, and rapists—people whose inner life and capacity for reflection were either atrophied or nonexistent. The French tradition of psychological analysis, in which an intelligent protagonist, like "la Princesse de Clèves" or Adolphe or Julien Sorel or Swann, reflects and comments on his environment and his experiences, no longer seemed suited for the type of novel being written by these "new" American novelists. Invariably the French protagonist was supremely intelligent. Even though he may be the victim of passion or of social forces and a destiny beyond his control he was at least capable of reflecting on the nature and quality of his experience. When the French began reading the American novel they were fascinated by the absence of such analysis. Sartre assures us, for instance, that *L'Etranger* would not exist, as we know it, if Camus had not read *The Sun Also Rises*. Sartre insists, however, that whereas Hemingway, who writes what he sees, is only obeying his temperament when he uses short, disjointed sentences, Camus, who imitates the Hemingway style, does so consciously and deliberately because its very emptiness best expresses the philosophical experience of the "absurd." [20] Hence the apparent discrepancy between Part I and Part II of *L'Etranger*. Part I copies the objectivity of the "style américain," whereas the moment Meursault (in prison) begins to reflect on the human condition Camus must return to the French tradition of analysis. The fact that Meursault is capable of such reflection means that he is not unintelligent and by implication indicates how much has deliberately been "left out" of Part I. Meursault remains intelligent in the tradition of French analysis. American novels like *The Sound and the Fury* or *Of Mice and Men* do not give us this duality in the same personage. We could not expect Faulkner's Benjy or Steinbeck's Lennie to undertake Meursault's metamorphosis. Mathias and the jealous husband are therefore more authentic imitations of the American "type" than was Meursault.

Faulkner's dislocation of time finds its echo in Simone de Beauvoir's *Le Sang des autres*. Sartre's *Le Sursis* is a deliberate imitation of Dos Passos' "objectivity" and "simultaneity." Henri Peyre, in *New French Writing* (New York: Grove, 1961), describes Claude Simons' book *L'Herbe* as "a funereal symphony of characters who look back upon their whole lives 'as they lie dying.'" Robbe-Grillet's dislocation of time and the tension of his novels, and Butor's preoccupation with time and subjectivity (while close to Joyce or Proust) reveal Faulkner's considerable influence.

One of the factors which the American novel has in common with the movies and which the novel of analysis does not, as Magny points out in her book on *L'Age du Roman Américain*, is its objectivity, the immediacy of its images, and the readiness with which plot and dialogue can be transposed from novel into film. The American novel, like the movies, tries to show rather than to tell. The tragic end of Joey Goodwin in *Sanctuary*, burned alive for a crime he did not commit, needs no commentary. Authorial comment would only weaken the shock impact. This is what Magny calls the art of ellipse so typical of certain American novels and inevitably present in the movies. Also, Faulkner does not describe Temple Drake's rape or Tommy's murder for the same reason that Robbe-Grillet does not describe Jacqueline's death. Aesthetically, this lack of information helps to build suspense. It is with painful slowness that *Light in August* reveals Joe Christmas' crime and the fact that he has negro blood.

Dos Passos' behaviorism and objectivity, his "camera eye," Faulkner's elliptical narrative, Hemingway's simple direct style devoid of analysis all find their counterpart in the movies. The American novel, before the French, was quick to sense the inherent literary possibilities of a film technique. Along with the point-of-view preoccupations of James, Lubbock, Wharton, Gide, and many others, the film has been stressing, as forcefully as the novel, the need to limit the point of view in time and space. This restriction of the camera's ubiquity means that its Editorial Omniscience is also suspect. The movies themselves seem conscious of the fact that this is an "age of suspicion."

The restriction in the point of view, the objectivism, and the "montage" of Robbe-Grillet's art forces the reader to recreate the experience of a sex maniac, a jealous husband, or of a personality breakdown, and in so doing to experience, as Eisenstein states, the dynamic process of the emergence and assembly of the image as it was experienced by the author or by the character of a particular novel. Freud's discussion of the dream sequence corresponds to the objectification of thought (conscious or unconscious) which is, in essence, the basis of Robbe-Grillet's narrative technique. His art work is, therefore, an experiment which, if it involves the reader (many still proclaim absolute boredom in reading Robbe-Grillet), is capable of giving him insight into behavior patterns which, until recently, was the exclusive domain of clinical psychology. By stressing the pathological Freud claimed to shed light on the "normal" processes of our affective life. Mathias' pathological dislocation of reality in terms of memory or fantasy gives the reader insight into his own day-dreaming processes. This day-dream, stimulated by external objects and events, Robbe-Grillet calls the "inner film" of the mind's eye. His narrative description projects this "inner film" onto the landscape as though the process were occurring outside of the character's imagination. Thought has now been objectified; it has been rendered visible. Material reality then becomes the thought's hieroglyph and is therefore ready to be filmed. "Ciné-roman," the language of the film and of the novel, has almost fused into a new genre using elements of both arts in order to blend the subjective and the objective reality of man into the higher synthesis of the surreal.

IN AN INTERVIEW published in *Le Monde*[1] Alain Robbe-Grillet says, in spite of all the critical articles about the objectivism of his novels, that the "subjectivity" of the protagonists is the main characteristic of *Le Voyeur* and *La Jalousie*.

This subjectivity is manifest in the way the travelling salesman and the nameless husband interact with their environment. In fact, their particular world is visible only in terms of a compulsive sexuality (Mathias), or of an equally compulsive jealousy (the nameless husband). Reality, for each of the protagonists, exists in the present, and consists of past, immediate, or fantasy images juxtaposed or superimposed in such a way as to reproduce conscious processes of thought or the psychic evolutions of the subconscious. These mechanisms of thought or feeling are objectified into images and things which, due to the special selectivity of human subjectivity, weave an irrevocable pattern of perverted murder by a sex maniac or the spying activities of a jealous husband. The selectivity is, of course, the author's too, so that the reader who is aware of the difference between geometric objects and "contaminated" objects always "sees" more than the protagonist does. What the reader "sees" on the one hand, is the inner film of the protagonist's mind caught under the "lens" of compulsive behavior patterns, and on the other, the imposed authorial "distance" of a neutral décor.

The subjectivity and selectivity of the protagonist depend on a specific personality derangement. Mathias is a sex pervert with schizoid tendencies, while the nameless husband is deliriously jealous. These two men see and react only to those aspects of their environment which are meaningful in terms of their psychological distress. The fact that Robbe-Grillet does not analyze their emotions in no way negates this subjectivity of theirs. The reader, instead of the novelist, must be the analyst: the reader must identify himself with the psychic continuum of these two deranged personalities yet, like the analyst, maintain a distance from it; the reader must see what the characters see and, if he does, the reader will realize that the apparently incoherent jumps in time-space, that the bizarre juxtaposition of objects and events follow a rigorous Freudian determinism. What is seen by each protagonist will depend upon the manner in which compulsion, regression, and free association are manifesting themselves. Robbe-Grillet's artistic technique is an extreme objectification or objectivism which is the reflection of the subjective world of these two protagonists as well as his own. These two novels, then, are a synthesis of the objective and the subjective. "Les objets seront 'là' avant d'être 'quelque chose,'" says Robbe-Grillet;[2] and if objects have meaning it is not due to any inherent qualities in them but to the way the author presents them and to the way in which Mathias and the jealous husband react to them and the associations which these objects evoke in their mind's eye.

The extreme subjectivity of these two men is not difficult to demonstrate. The moment the reader can adjust to the deranged world of Mathias or the jealous husband he begins to see as they "see"; he begins to understand how their deranged minds are operating. Let us take one of Mathias' more obvious hallucinations: in the beginning of Part II of *Le Voyeur* Mathias has just killed Jacqueline, the thirteen-year-old girl, and he is back on the road where he sees the crushed carcass of a dead frog or toad. This frog metamorphoses into a sea gull which is then seen flying overhead. In *La Jalousie* the husband's jealousy prompts him to associate the noise made by the mandibles of a centipede with the electric static of a comb, and finally, with the sound of fire. These two examples of the subjective objectification of images and associations must, I think, be understood in terms of a surrealistic juxtaposition which also lends itself to the depth of meaning of a Freudian interpretation.

The sea gull flying over Mathias' head in patterns of eight is a constant reminder (within the framework of this novel) of Mathias' compulsive psychosexual infantilism. The frog with its "open thighs, arms forming a cross" must surely remind the reader of the victim Jacqueline who has previously been described in terms not unlike these. The elongated shadow of a kilometer marker (phallic symbol?) is juxtaposed with and points towards the dead frog only a few inches away from the tip of the shadow. Mathias need not be conscious of any symbolism as long as the reader is, and, if the reader makes the connection between these apparently unconnected objects then he is undergoing a surrealistic experience which depends for its impact, as Breton says, on the living synthesis of the real and the unreal. Lautréamont's famous example of the fortuitous encounter on a dissecting table of a sewing machine and an umbrella is the elaboration of an identical process. Behind this apparently baroque and incoherent affabulation, psychoanalysts claim to have discovered the female and male symbols and a bed. Are not the elongated shadow and the spread legs of the frog an even more suggestive symbol? Will not the subconscious (Mathias' in this case) juxtapose disparate elements for the satisfaction of its needs? In *La Jalousie* the "narrator" listens to the song of one of the native workmen. This song, which the workman sings in bits and snatches, stopping, then resuming, with no apparent rhythmic or musical pattern to govern its sequence is like the deep flow of the river (man's subconscious?) which follows the laws of its own logic and inner necessity: "Yet these repetitions, these minute variants, these excisions, these regressions, may give rise to hardly discernible modifications leading, in the long run, to distances far from the point of departure" (*La Jalousie*, p. 101). This quotation which is Robbe-Grillet's oblique allusion to the technique of his novel duplicates, in turn, the internal rhythm of the husband's jealous psyche which dislocates chronological time for the satisfaction of its inner emotional time sequence.

Readers of *La Jalousie* will remember how the husband's imagination and memory focus repetitively on the centipede and on its stain on the wall. When A... and Franck do not return on time from their trip to the city, we can expect the husband's jealous anxiety to dwell on the reasons for their delay and, insomuch as he has reason to believe that there is a clandestine relationship between them, his morbid imagination sees A... combing her hair, A... and Franck in bed, and A... and Franck crashing into a tree. The various artistic and symbolic levels of this sequence are in themselves interesting, but what is immediately *à propos* is the transition from centipede to comb to fire in terms of image as well as time sequence. In *Le Voyeur* we had a frog and a shadow on the road. Now we have three different and apparently equally inappropriate objects juxtaposed in similar fashion. Everything becomes clear, however, if we accept the centipede as the objective correlative of the husband's jealousy. The reader will also remember the many sensuous descriptions of A... combing her wavy black hair, a preoccupation which in itself is extremely logical, since A... is the immediate concern of the husband's jealousy.

The spot of the centipede on the wall is the imperfection which jealousy casts on his personality makeup. Will he not try desperately to erase this spot at a critical moment? His deranged senses imagine the automobile accident of A... and Franck as a sexual climax in bed and also, quite probably, as a homicidal wish-fulfillment. The crackling sounds made by mandibles, a comb, and fire, therefore, are capable of evoking an entire sequence whose impact on the reader must again be described as surrealistic. The association of these images depends upon the libidinal drive of the unconscious (the jealous husband's in this case) which, the surrealists claim, is the source of all such juxtapositions. Do they not say that the greater the dissimilarity of the juxtaposed objects the greater the beauty? Are not the images of surrealism, whose impact depends not upon their analysis but upon the "bringing together of two more or less distant realities," an objectification of the subconscious? And did not Breton seek the active synthesis of the objective and the subjective in terms of what he called "le hasard objectif" (objective chance)? The great role of surrealism, according to Breton, is to capture "the projected film of word-images which surge forth from their engulfed depths." These words might have been used by Robbe-Grillet himself to describe an aspect of his own aesthetic doctrine.[3]

Since the surrealists were using the theories of Freudian determinism for an elaboration of "related" images they were convinced that the creative genius would be able to tap significant layers of the human subconscious out of which would come universal (hence significant) juxtapositions capable of involving the reader's (or the spectator's in the case of painting) psyche. The truth of these images was equated with beauty but it was not a question of arbitrarily regrouping words or images. Breton himself describes it as the artist's capacity to create his own hallucinations, not as pure delirium, but as an exploration of delirium. The spontaneous recording of images surging forth from the subconscious constitutes the element of "truth" the surrealists were pursuing. Has not Robbe-Grillet created two fictional characters whose psyches he uses for a voluntary exploration of delirium? Robbe-Grillet's own description of the husband, whose "distrust borders on delirium," is perhaps not insignificant.[4] What really matters, however, in spite of the differences I have indicated, is the artistic synthesis which Robbe-Grillet has devised of the objective and the subjective—of material reality and the inner psychic "reality" of man. The reader sees the synthesis of these two realities (hence the word "higher") through the eyes of the protagonist. The author is dealing with the protagonist's subconscious. But the descriptions themselves obviously will come from the imagination and style of the author. The higher synthesis then must depend on the "spark" of insight generated by the author through the protagonist but realized by the reader. Insomuch as this blend of the objective and the subjective was the ultimate goal of the surrealists and insomuch as the objective exploration of Mathias' and the jealous husband's psyche illustrate how the mind works under certain conditions of stress, then the reader, by virtue of his insight into the "related distance" of the juxtapositions, understands "the truth" about certain interrelationships—that centipede, woman's hair, and fire represent the "inner film" of the husband's jealousy. The inner necessity of jealousy is responsible for this incongruous juxtaposition. The plausibility of bringing together distant yet related images is now explainable in terms of a certain passion. The "truth" which relates these images *is* jealousy. This is, I suppose, in addition to the "neutral" description of objects, what Robbe-Grillet meant when he said that *Les Gommes* was a scientific novel.[5] "We are present," said the surrealists, "for the magnificent honeymoon of science and the imagination."

A big difference between a novel like *Le Voyeur* and *Nadja* comes from the detachment of the novelist. *Nadja* was essentially an autobiographical experience narrated in the first person. Breton makes no attempt to camouflage this fact and the reader cannot or does not make a real synthesis between the "hasard objectif"(s) and Breton's subconscious. *Nadja* as a work of art seems to lack the directive force, the compulsive inner necessity, which, for instance, makes the incongruous imagery of the jealous husband plausible. In Robbe-Grillet's two novels the way is clear for such a synthesis. We know after so many pages of *Le Voyeur* that Mathias' sexuality is a predisposing factor. This we infer, for the most part, from his dreamlike trances, events, coincidences, and recognitions which, for him, represent a cumulative series of "hasards objectifs." The manner in which he animates a movie poster clearly illustrates his relationship to the external environment (p. 45): "On the violently colored poster, a colossus of a man, in Renaissance clothes, was holding a young person dressed in a kind of long pale chemise. On her bosom, with one hand, he had immobilized her two wrists. Her head and face were partly averted in an effort to ward off her assailant and her long flowing blond hair reached to the ground." The altered contents of this "imagination," as Robbe-Grillet calls it, will appear frequently as a blend of reality and fantasy until they are transfigured into Mathias' sadistic crime—a crime which will reproduce all of the violence previously imagined as well as seen.

Therefore, when figure eights, rusty pitons, cigarettes, a statue to the dead, and the fragile neck of a young girl are associated, a pattern emerges which is clearly a reflection of Mathias' unconscious selectivity. The reader makes the necessary synthesis between predisposing and precipitating factors, he "sees the truth" of the surrealistic juxtaposition as it is revealed by the protagonist's "automatic" associations. This experience is at the same time an aesthetic satisfaction for the reader and an increase in knowledge if, as one might assume, insight into the workings of the subconscious represents some kind of knowledge.

There is evidence to suggest that the derangement of the senses, when analyzed, is capable of eliciting such insight. At least Rimbaud's famous "Lettre du Voyant" seems to indicate that this is so. The images which the soul "sees" after it has deliberately made itself monstrous, if faithfully recorded, have all the elements of a scientific experiment. The hallucinations of the *Bateau Ivre*, which were part of Rimbaud's revolt against stifling social values (his mother's as well as society's), are the visions of such an experiment. And was he not one of the fathers of surrealism (a youthful one to be sure) when he said that he imagined factories in the sky in the place of clouds? And was not his method of nonanalytic juxtaposition of images and events, as in the poem "Ornières," an indication of the system the surrealists were to follow in exploring (nonanalytically) the raw images of the subconscious? Rimbaud's *voyant* however has given way to Robbe-Grillet's *voyeur* who does not comprehend the meaning of his visions. Hence the need for stylistic synthesis—the fusing of the protagonist's "inner" and "outer" worlds in terms of *one* objectified description—which brings Robbe-Grillet's novels out of the realm of an ordinary case-study in fictional form into the realm of art. It is this synthesis which enables the reader to understand the meaning of what Max Ernst in *Position* describes as the "coupling of two apparently incompatible realities in a situation or relationship which apparently does not suit them." Insomuch as these two novels of Robbe-Grillet explain this process and insomuch as they illustrate how the most tangible objectivity can relate to the most extreme subjectivity they fulfill one of the basic goals of the surrealistic experiment.

Dans le labyrinthe represents a further elaboration of surrealism in Robbe-Grillet's work. In it dream and reality, as Breton suggests, are "communicating vases" through which the events of one dimension correspond to events in another. The doctor-narrator breaks down the usual distinction between the objective picture of "The Defeat of Reichenfels" and the subjective imagination of man and plunges himself and the reader into a dream in which the immediate reality of time and space is being experienced in two different centuries. It is this kind of surreality, more real because it is a heightened perception of the possible, which gives fantastic creations their legitimate expression as art. The imagination of the doctor, isolated in his room, is the creative spark, the link between an event ("The Defeat of Reichenfels") of the previous century, represented pictorially, and the immediacy of a personal experience which he cannot grasp *in toto* but which he is free to reconstruct. The enemy is in the streets of the city, the doctor has time on his hands and, as he reflects on the circumstances which may have led to the death of the soldier, his imagination blends imperceptibly with the picture on the wall, the barrier between dream and reality disappears as a super dream-reality recreates the possibilities inherent in two homologous situations.

L'Année dernière à Marienbad presents additional interesting parallels. The "château," which for Breton is one of the strongest of all surrealistic images, is the setting for a series of events and coincidences which, once more, will fuse the real and the imaginary into a new and heightened experience. In *Nuit du Tournesol* (*Night of the Sunflower*) Breton describes events which, eleven years later, were to be "mysteriously" fulfilled. He meets a woman whom he had described without even knowing her. Their relationship, their actions, their gestures, even "la couleur du temps" (the color of time) had been foreseen and described in their smallest details, affirms Breton. He explains this remarkable coincidence as a fulfillment of *desire*. It is this exteriorized desire which is, no doubt, capable of finding a person and reorganizing events in such a way as to correspond to the vision of an initial dream or the dictates of the subconscious. Thus, according to Breton, chance depends on "the encounter of an external causality and an internal finality, the manifestation of an exterior necessity which penetrates the human unconscious."

Robbe-Grillet turns this procedure around. Instead of re-creating the future, X re-creates the past. But X's endeavor is not a dream, nor is it the recording of his subconscious. He seems determined to "free" A from the rooms and the corridors of what Robbe-Grillet calls a "golden cage" and he is perfectly lucid in his pursuit of her. For the surrealists, the most efficient means of liberation is love, and indeed it is love which X seems to be offering A in his attempt to lure her away from the decadent world of the idle rich. The humanitarian impulse of Revolution was, we must not forget, one of the tenets of surrealism. Love itself was to be a revolutionary force. This "amour fou" (mad love), capable of breaking the barriers in which society has enclosed it, finds its fullest fruition in a kind of Gidean "disponibilité" (readiness for adventure) that helps it satisfy and realize the needs of the inner self. X shows A a bracelet which she allegedly gave him "last year" and he then shows her a picture of herself again allegedly taken "last year." His voice re-creates for the viewer, in A's and in X's imagination, the same halls, the same formal gardens, the same statues in which and around which, he claims, they met and where their love developed. A at first mockingly says that of course it must have been "par hasard" ("by chance"—that objective chance so essential for surrealism), but as X's insistence seems to supply proof after proof, demonstrating a previous encounter, her certitude begins to waver. As in Aragon's *Le Paysan de Paris* (*The Peasant of Paris*) X has sought the marvels of daily chance meetings and chance events which, combined with "the reality of" a fictitious past will transform daily reality. X succeeds in confusing A and perhaps in making her love him. The places and events he describes in the past bear a striking resemblance to the gardens and events of the present. A's flashbacks will reveal a progressive inability to distinguish between past and present, between the real and the unreal.

"Images think for me," explained Paul Eluard in "Défense de savoir." X's words are a catalyst for A's images projected on the screen. In this sense he is depending on the creative role of language to supply the proper scenes in A's imagination. What the spectator sees in the movie is the force of the sudden unexpected image as it is recorded in the imagination of A or of X. The hypnotic effect is so strong, the evidence of her surroundings in which she finds herself with X is so overwhelming, that she comes to doubt the authentic nature of her memory. Thus the nocturnal dream sequence in the garden is the climax of A's fear but also of her desire. This moment is for the viewer (even though perhaps not for A) a moment of insight during which A's fear—her fusion of reality and fantasy as well as of past and present—is objectified into the violence of the scene. Thunder strikes as she says "pour l'amour de moi," and as she pleads with X to flee. The clap of thunder is the "coup de foudre," appropriately ambiguous in French for love at first sight. X leaps for safety as the stone railing crumbles. He is then "seen" in a lifeless heap on the ground.

The spectator now feels reasonably certain that A will leave M. And indeed when she does leave with X the whole notion of the "déjà vu" has been materialized. The distinction between the real and the imaginary has broken down. What was imaginary for "last year" has become real now. Every event and every coincidence is a meticulous reproduction of X's ingenious determination to possess A and perhaps, at the same time, to affirm his own creative freedom.

This experience is for A analogous to the coincidence Breton describes in *Nuit du Tournesol*. For the events of the present which correspond to "last year at Marienbad" appear to be a series of remarkable "hasards objectifs" whose evidence and intensity she cannot deny. This will perhaps explain the look of despair she and her husband exchange near the end of the movie when it must be evident to both of them that they are lost to each other.

If M is the embodiement of the decadence of a rich aristocracy, then X's determination to free A through love moves even more forcefully towards the revolutionary aspect of surrealism. But love is only a "porte étroite" (a strait gate) on the road to Revolution which, on the one hand, was to be the community of men and, on the other, the creation, as Lautréamont said, of poetry by all. This double mission of surrealism, to transform the world and thereby change life depends for its success on the objectification of desire. X objectifies his desire as things of his environment. He disguises his desire by projecting it and succeeds finally in trapping A in "the parc of this hotel which was a kind of garden in the French manner, without a tree, without a flower, without vegetation of any kind. . . . Gravel stone, marble, the straight line, delineated its rigid spaces. It seemed at first impossible to lose oneself in it . . . at first . . . along the rectangular paths, between the inanimate gestures of statues and the granit slabs" (*L'Année dernière à Marienbad*, p. 172). But X is not a true surrealistic hero. He is a false savior goaded by some inner demonic necessity. The violent decor of A's imagination is not a liberation (the difference between the text and the movie is here paramount) but an enslavement. Instead of offering her a series of "hasards objectifs" which correspond to her inner necessity, X offers her a fictitious past (Robbe-Grillet's assertion that they have never met is here significant) which only leads her to doubt herself. She is not in love with him. She is the prisoner of the fiction X has woven about her. She is the prisoner of the very objects which constitute this fiction. A is even incapable of choice. We presume that if she were really in love with X she would not have asked for the midnight reprieve, whereby she asks X or M to choose for her. M chooses not to come on time and she leaves with X. The episode ends in the formal gardens with X's final words echoing in the night: "Where you were now already in the process of losing yourself, forever, in the tranquil night, alone with me."

L'Année dernière à Marienbad is, once again, a demonstration of Robbe-Grillet's theory of the alienation of self. A's pathological fear seems to stem not so much from M, who always treats her with extreme gentleness, but from X's relentless pursuit. She continuously tries to evade him, he is continuously after her and she is forever saying "laissez-moi, laissez-moi." This, we discover, is more than a coquettish "no." She is genuinely afraid and, not without justification, for X is forcing a reality on her which does not exist.

Marienbad then appears to be an experiment in which A is a human guinea pig and X a Protean grotesque of the doctor-narrator in *Dans le labyrinthe*. One presumes that A, unless she can escape from the enslavement to X or to things (primarily things—like bracelets, photographs, garden paths, and statues), may, like *Nadja*, become hopelessly mad. Unless, like the comedienne, at the beginning of the script she can say "this hope is now without object. The fear has passed, to lose such a tie, such a prison, such a lie" (p. 29). The contrast and the irony are not insignificant. Whereas A remains incapable of choosing between M and X, the comedienne deliberately says to the man on the stage: "Je suis à vous."

The play within the play is not only an aspect of the baroque and corresponds to the baroque ceiling of the hotel-château; it will also serve as a "déjà vu," a "déjà" heard, which will reinforce the whole surrealistic theme of objective chance. These baroque ceilings and interminable corridors will be like a "golden cage" from which X appears to be freeing her only to make her the prisoner of the formal gardens and the straight paths bordering the hedges and the frozen statues. This is a surrealism "à rebours" (against the grain) which Robbe-Grillet uses to demonstrate some men's dilemma and possible "tragedy." Not that the surrealists were the victims of this anthropocentrism. They were much too lucid for that. As Anna Balakian observes in her book on *Surrealism,*[6] it was the influence of Freud and Hegel that enables them to combat the narcissism of those who obliterate the world by incorporating themselves in it. In *Le Voyeur,* Mathias, an isolated being, and an unconscious narcissist, finds his inner self reflected in everything he sees. He is the unconscious victim of a world he has humanized and which in turn precipitates his crime. He has been trapped by things in the same manner that A has and that Wallas has.

Marienbad is then a tragedy played out in the silent, empty, dismal corridors of the hotel-château. A is the heroine, X is the villain who pursues her through the labyrinth of corridors and emotions while Robbe-Grillet demonstrates, once more, the consequences of what we may now call "neo-tragic complicity."

8   CONCLUSION

ROMANTICISM HAS PASSED full cycle. Madame de Staël's notion that man's great achievements are due to his feeling of an incomplete destiny finds its final dying echo in that most prehensile tail of the romantic movement—existentialism.

The *Voices of Silence*, as Malraux calls them, are the voices of all those artists who, obsessed with time and death, have created works of art in an attempt to impose a human stamp on the face of an impersonal destiny. Such works of art are born of the anguish of contingency—an art which rises out of man's challenge to death. This "chant sacré" is the only means at man's disposal with which to overcome the forces of destiny—of giving significance to an "absurd" world.[1]

Camus' tribute to Malraux (at the time of his Nobel speech in Stockholm) reveals the indebtedness of the younger "existentialists" to the man who "had shown the way." Tragedy, action, commitment became literary by-words for a whole generation raised on existentialist dogma. The "new novel," however, in spite of its indebtedness to the movement, seems determined to remain aloof from the social and political commitment of existentialism. "The only commitment possible, for the writer," says Robbe-Grillet, "is literature."[2]

In *Les Voix du silence* Malraux, the art critic, stresses man's ability to rise above death and above the human condition through art. Sartre the philosopher wants man, in his individual choice, to choose as though he were choosing for all men. His artistic spokesmen stress choice and "engagement" as a means of liberating man from the determinism of his destiny. Camus the essayist celebrates man's "non" as a positive affirmation of "l'homme révolté" who, in rebellion against evil, says "I choose, therefore we are." All of these devices, art criticism, the philosophic tract, the essay are a way of giving audible expression to the meaning of their novels. The meaning of the "existential" novel is further reinforced either by editorial intrusion in the traditional manner or by a first person narrative spokesman for the author. Robbe-Grillet, like his precursors, has written articles clarifying the "content" of his novels, but the technique of his novels is so unusual and the need for transforming the visible picture into intelligible content so new (perhaps not so new but used in a strikingly different manner) that critics have made the mistake of assuming that there is no meaning in his novels and that they are pure technique. The reading public does not yet understand that, within the context of Robbe-Grillet's work, objects, posters, photographs, and pictures, like a painting, have meaning which the reader who "sees" must translate. The composite "picture" of a novel may depend for its meaning on the novel's allegorical setting.

Les Gommes is, in this sense an interim novel. It represents Robbe-Grillet's attempt to adapt Greek tragedy to a Freudian detective story. The Sophoclean epigraph, "Time which watches over everything, has given the solution in spite of you," while relating the novel to the more ponderous tradition of man's fate by no means imbues Wallas with the grandeur of Oedipus. What fascinates us in *Oedipus the King* is the simultaneous consciousness of man's servitude in relation to his indomitable determination to impose himself on destiny. The task is futile, as the *Myth of Sisyphus* indicates; yet man's greatness, if we may use this term, derives precisely from his attempt to impose a human accent on these forces. Wallas is not a "tragic" hero in the normally accepted sense of the word.

His servitude to his complex and to things is complete. He has none of the dignity of consciousness Sophocles or Malraux insist upon. He is not even conscious that it is *his* problem which is in the balance. Nor is Sophocles' Oedipus. But Oedipus' determination to get to the root of the matter and rid his nation of the pestilence has a magnitude which appeals to the imagination. Wallas' search for a petty assassin shows how far tragedy has fallen from its triumphant past. Of course, kings have fallen too, and if modern literature is about the problems of the petty bourgeois, everyman (H.C.E. as Joyce calls him), you or me, this transformation is due, I suppose, to what Ortega describes as "the revolt of the masses." This leveling process, this democratization of existence has taken the "kick" out of tragedy. Can we really blame the spectator or the reader for not getting excited about the tragedy of an anonymous being whom he has never met or heard about. The equanimity with which we read about murders, accidents, and the daily procession of death across the front pages of our newspapers provide, indeed, a paltry equivalent for the tragedies of kings, gods, and emperors.

The only tragedy a modern man *can* get excited about is his own. This is the theme of Berger in *Les Noyers de L'Altenburg,* of Roquentin in *La Nausée,* and of Meursault in *L'Etranger.* This is the topic of Kafka's novels and of Beckett's cripples. Don Juanism and Faustism have been personalized. If Sarraute is right, and if the modern avant-garde writer no longer feels comfortable in creating a Julien Sorel or a Raskolnikov, then the trend towards the anonymous protagonist, for whom the reader can substitute his own name, is a logical and significant trend. Kafka's K., Sarraute's nameless personages, Robbe-Grillet's initials represent these authors' determination, using every technical means, to force the attention and active participation of the reader. The restriction of the point of view, the absence of analysis, and the objectification of emotion enable the reader to project *himself* into the action of the novel more fully than was possible before.

But the meanings of tragedy have changed. To say that

man is subservient to destiny is, of course, not very helpful, since destiny manifests itself in many different ways.
Destiny will wear the mask a particular author wishes to
give it. Destiny personalized may, as with Adam or
Prometheus, represent a revolt against God or the gods.
Or, with Proust, tragedy may be represented as a fight
against Time. Or, as with Vigny, tragedy may be marked
as a struggle against "Nature." Tolstoy may give destiny
historical dimensions while Stendhal, Balzac, and Zola
may describe man's struggle against social forces which
are perceived as evil. Dos Passos attacks the big city and
the machine while Faulkner's sense of tragedy may be, as
Magny points out, a "theological inversion." [3] Tragedy
for Malraux, Sartre, and Camus stems from the very act
of living and being born.

Tragedy is not merely the imposition of external factors
but depends, for its particular manifestation, on the personality structure of one man—that is, all those predisposing factors which, as with Temple Drake, explain her
passive role with Popeye. If the subconscious is part of our
basic personality structure and is formed of residual experiences—childhood memories, desires, frustrations, guilt,
conflicts, repressions, etc.—then these forces will operate
on the individual in strange and often unpredictable ways.
Thus Temple's revolt, which is in part her character,
forces destiny, surprises the reader, and leaves him wonder-
ing why a "nice" girl like her should end up in a brothel.
Faulkner in *Sanctuary* provides no psychological analysis
in the manner of Proust, precisely because Temple is incapable of such descriptive insight. But Faulkner does
provide enough family and social clues, at least, to make
her behavior plausible. It is the reader's task, if he can, to
explain this plausibility. The "new novel's" creation of a
neo-detective genre (*Les Gommes*, *L'Emploi du temps*,
Le Vent) is a substitute for the traditional form of
psychological analysis or Editorial Omniscience.

But if writers like Robbe-Grillet, Butor, and Simon
have borrowed heavily from the detective story, the "new
novel" owes as much, perhaps, to *Madame Bovary*, *La*

Porte Etroite, and *L'Immoraliste.* Gide in his preface to *La Tentative amoureuse,* and echoing Flaubert, affirms that verisimilitude in fiction depends on the author's insight into the inner psychological necessity of his protagonists. The novel will then unfold around an error, a defect in the hero's personality makeup, which leads him or her consistently to deform reality. It is this pathology of character which will ultimately be responsible for the dénouement of the novel. The discrepancy between Emma's romantic nature and the ugliness of her daily reality will, eventually, lead her to suicide. Alissa's inability to reconcile her mother's infidelity in marriage leads Alissa to reject Jérome and seek refuge in dubious religious austerity. Michel's inability to tolerate the slightest stain of an imperfection (his wife's T.B.) when combined with a Nietzschean "disponibilité" will lead him to "sacrifice" Marceline. Thus two novels, apparently as antipodal as *L'Immoraliste* and *La Porte Etroite,* represent Gide's search for meaning and the purgation of his own problem. The destiny of Michel and Alissa was potentially Gide's destiny. The smothering of all the rosebuds except one culminates in the flowering of a deformed religious zeal or in an equally deformed narcissism. Wallas' Oedipus complex, Mathias' psychosexual infantilism, the husband's jealousy belong to an analogous elaboration of the creative process.

But aside from such "anatomies" what is the new novel trying to say? With Simon the reader comes to recognize the multiplicity, proliferation, and ambiguity of life; with Sarraute the reader develops a hyperconscious recognition that conversation, dialogue, and words are only the visible part of an iceberg—that beneath the surface of audible expression there is a subconversational world which may or may not correspond to our verbal utterances; with Butor the novel becomes a search for itself and the characters (unlike those of Robbe-Grillet) move from uncertainty to certainty or to new and meaningful insights. Jacques Revel, unlike Wallas, does extricate himself from the symbolic labyrinth. Butor's characters, therefore, achieve a liberation which Robbe-Grillet's do not. Butor creates novels which open upon themselves and endow his personages with a new creative freedom. Robbe-Grillet's personages are closed upon themselves and their tragedy derives not only from their inner pathology, that error in their personality makeup, but finally, and inevitably, from their inability to recognize the fundamental distance between themselves and objects. Objects act as catalysts and the resultant complicity further strengthens the prison of their emotions.

This tragedy, which stresses the fact that the tragic element in man is to be found within himself, though not new, has found a new means of expression. *La Jalousie*, for instance, represents a heightened intensity of emotion verging on the poetic. The "new man" Robbe-Grillet refers to in his essay "nouveau roman—homme nouveau" will be, unlike the jealous husband, an integrated being. Robbe-Grillet's characters are all schizoids. Their conscious and subconscious lives operate on different levels and it is precisely this separation which leads Wallas and Mathias to murder. The alienation of self stems from the fact that man can and does infuse objects with human meaning. This process is inevitable, no doubt, and all of us use it. The danger, however, derives from any subservience to such objects. (Things precipitate Meursault's senseless crime and Roquentin's "nausea.") The novel, as Robbe-Grillet envisages it, is a demonstration of what happens to those who refuse to accept the "distance" between themselves and the external world. This complicity is a prison which, due to unresolved psychological complexes, makes people project human meaning into "neutral" objects. These objects, in turn, influence behavior; they are the mirrors of subconscious desire, fear, anxiety which act cumulatively, heighten tension, and exercise reciprocal action. The novel of the future, as Robbe-Grillet defines it, is one which will explore all the possible facets and manifestations of such "tragic complicity."

But the avowed purpose of the modern novel, when compared with the novel of the past, seems to have changed less than its technique. If Hardy interrupts the narrative to tell the reader that Tess is at fault in anthropomorphizing nature, so does Robbe-Grillet. It is the nature of the intrusion rather than its purpose which has changed so radically. Robbe-Grillet has evolved a unique system which incorporates authorial judgment of characters while seeming to remain outside the story. He therefore combines Selective Omniscience with Editorial Omniscience as unnamed variations of a character's perceptions and the author's style.

Robbe-Grillet's imitators, however, have borrowed his technical innovations but not his purpose. Daniel Castelain's *Une Rencontre improbable* is a painfully self-conscious version of the "creative" possibilities inherent in *Dans le labyrinthe*. Robbe-Grillet's and Ricardou's techniques are so similar that isolated passages from one author could be mistaken for those of the other. Ricardou, however, does not use the basic structure of "tragic complicity." Another novel, *Composition No 1*, by Marc Saporta, is typical of the limitations of a superficial imposition of technique. It has 150 pages which, once you have read them, may be shuffled and read, then reshuffled and reread endlessly in an always newly recurring order. Each page represents a unit of experience which may be read as reality or fantasy and hence as present, past, or future. This novel is, therefore, the first true literary equivalent of nonobjective painting. If a nonobjective painting is capable of meaning all things to all viewers, then *Composition No 1* (the very title is indicative) is at the same time full of meaning and devoid of meaning. Each reshuffling will present a new and completely gratuitous order of events with which the reader's imagination, as in *Finnegans Wake*, can play *ad infinitum*. This reminds us of Raymond Queneau's tour de force *Cent mille milliards de poèmes*. But is not such artistic nihilism reminiscent of Dada and are such literary efforts really more significant than an occasional amusing parlor game?

That such efforts represent the revolt of man against the pressures of a modern industrial civilization or against the fragmentation of human time by the arbitrary demands of a socially imposed clock time is possible. *Composition No 1* (all possibilities are relevant) might even be interpreted as the perfect mirror of an arbitrary and absurd Universe. But it lacks focus. Robbe-Grillet's dislocation of time-space is not arbitrary. It fulfills the pathological necessity of jealousy, fear, etc. If our inner needs could order *Composition No 1* this novel would be satisfactory. But it is not, because man's psychological activity and behavior are not arbitrary. Events may appear gratuitous, but the ordering of the self in relation to them never is. Mathias' compulsion orders a sequence of events which lead him inevitably to murder.

Claude Ollier's *La Mise en scène* (*The Setting*, 1958) is an interesting amalgamation of Robbe-Grillet and Butor. It is about the journey of a young French engineer to a remote Arab village in North Africa where he is to prepare for the opening of a mine. At each stage of the journey the hero uncovers events in the life of a predecessor which have a curious and threatening parallelism to his own "adventure." The descriptive technique is typical of Robbe-Grillet's "new realism." Like Jacques Revel, who escapes from the labyrinth of Bleston which threatens to destroy him, the mining engineer refuses involvement with a native girl and a vengeful Arab in spite of "le génie du lieu" (as Butor would call it). Ollier's talent is unmistakable. His novel is the fascinating description of a character who can resist the complicity of things and events.

L'Emploi du temps, though a pseudo-detective novel, is about the effect of things or places on the human psyche. Butor, like Robbe-Grillet, has manipulated in his own original way the triangular relationship which exists between the author, the reader, and the characters of a novel. In fact *L'Emploi du temps* uses the detective novel structure and Greek motif of *Les Gommes* and superimposes it upon the labyrinthine structure of Bleston. Butor's use of the city as a destructive force finds its antecedents, of course, in the work of Joyce and Dos

Passos. The very inertia of Bleston's monotony is a laby-rinth, the two sisters in the novel are Phaedra and Ariadne, while the journal Jacques Revel is writing is the thread which allows him to reorient himself and emerge from the maze. The stained-glass window and the tapes-tries, like the Oedipus motif in *Les Gommes*, are the mythological objectification of its modern thematic coun-terpart.

As a scientist, Robbe-Grillet seems to believe in the relativity of perception and experience, whereas Butor does not. For Butor, if man is incapable of resolving the Sphinx's riddle, it is not because truth or reality is relative, but because reality in its depths is too mysterious to be deciphered. On the other hand, Jacques Revel and the husband in *La Modification*, by their analysis, their reflec-tive processes, and their search for a solution do find answers to their particular dilemmas. Butor's novels are therefore primarily in the tradition of French analysis, and his personages, typically, have more insight into their activities (even if Jacques Revel must write a journal to achieve insight) than Robbe-Grillet's sick, jealous, fever-wracked, and scared victims.

Unlike Robbe-Grillet who owes much to surrealism, Butor is a disciple not only of Joyce, but of Mallarmé. Each event in Butor's novels is framed, reinforced, and extended by the multiplicity of all other events contingent on the past or on the future. His imagery, like that of the symbolists, tends to be more abstract in meaning and less defined in connotation than Robbe-Grillet's. His lan-guage suggests moods rather than visions. It is not as con-crete in shape and color, in texture and intent as the vocabulary of Robbe-Grillet or of the surrealists who use language to define objects with a precision verging on the scientific.

But in spite of their differences Robbe-Grillet, Butor, and Ollier all seem to be moving in the same direction. Their novels, in very specific and personal ways, can lead the reader out of the labyrinth of anthropomorphism. Robbe-Grillet's characters remain the prisoners of this "complicity." Butor's personages, generally speaking, find a way out. Ollier's mining engineer is alerted in time and so, he too, escapes. The "new novel" is, therefore, not pure technical virtuosity. It has a meaningful philosophical basis, a sound tradition, and talented writers. These new writers are redefining tragedy in the light of psychological and phenomenological thinking.

"Tragedy," as Roland Barthes says, "is but a means of accepting human misfortune, of subsuming human misery, and therefore of justifying it as necessary, as a kind of wisdom or purification. To reject this salvage operation and to seek out technical means not to yield treasonably to it (for nothing is more insidious than tragedy) is, in our time, a necessary undertaking." [4]

1—New Forms for Old

1. Alain Robbe-Grillet, "Notes sur la localisation et les déplacements du point de vue dans la description romanesque," *Revue des Lettres Modernes,* V (1958), 258.

2. Frederick Hoffman, *Samuel Beckett—The Language of Self* (Carbondale: Southern Illinois University Press, 1962), pp. 58–59.

3. *Ibid.,* pp. 67–68.

4. *Répertoire* (Paris: Editions de Minuit, 1960).

5. (Paris: Gallimard, 1956).

6. Norman Friedman, "Point of View in Fiction: The Development of a Critical Concept," *PMLA,* LXX (1955), 1170–72.

7. See Friedman, pp. 1160–84.

8. "Panorama d'une nouvelle littérature romanesque," *Esprit* (July–August 1958), 9.

9. *Yale French Studies—Midnight Novelists,* no. 24 (Summer 1959), 106.

2—The Existential Milieu

1. Julien Green, *Le Voyageur sur la terre* (Paris: Plon, 1930)—Livre de Poche, p. 74.

2. Alain Robbe-Grillet, "Le Réalisme, la psychologie, et l'avenir du roman," *Critique,* XII (1956), 699.

3. The French is "en imagination." "Des imagina-

tions" is the descriptive term Robbe-Grillet uses for his characters' mental operations.

4. Jorge Luis Borges, *Labyrinths* (New York: New Directions, 1962), p. 66.

5. See Bruce Morrissette, "Oedipus and Existentialism: *Les Gommes* of Robbe-Grillet," *Wisconsin Studies in Contemporary Literature,* I (1960), 43–73.

6. Jean-Paul Sartre, *La Nausée* (Paris: Gallimard, 1938)—Livre de Poche, pp. 184–85.

7. Alain Robbe-Grillet, "Nature, Humanisme, Tragédie," *NNRF,* October 1958.

3—A Novel of Objective Subjectivity: The Voyeur

1. Denise Bourdet, "Le Cas Robbe-Grillet," *La Revue de Paris,* LXVI (1959), 132.

2. Robert Champigny, "In Search of the Pure Récit," *The American Society Legion of Honor Magazine,* XXVII (Winter 1956/57), 338.

3. Roland Barthes, "Littérature littérale," *Critique,* XII (1955), 823.

4. "In Search of the Pure Récit," p. 339.

5. Ibid.

6. Alain Robbe-Grillet, "L'Anné dernière à Marienbad," *Réalités,* no. 184 (1961), 98.

7. As quoted by Claude Sarraute, "La Subjectivité est la caractéristique du roman contemporain," *Le Monde* (11–17 May 1961), p. 7.

8. "When I discovered Kafka and American literature written between the two wars," says Robbe-Grillet, "I had the feeling that I should advance in that direction." André Bourin, "Techniciens du roman," *Nouvelles Littéraires* (22 January 1959), p. 1.

9. Superficially, Robbe-Grillet's novels would seem to be detective stories since *Les Gommes* uses a detective, Wallas, to solve the alleged murder. In *Le Voyeur* a murder does take place, and the reader is, in essence, asked to solve the crime. In *La Jalousie* the spying husband and the reader act as accomplice detectives. In *Dans le labyrinthe,*

the reader is again asked to solve the meaning of the story. But Robbe-Grillet's novels do not fit the classic stereotype of detective novels or "whodunits." In the pure detective novel all are suspect, the murderer is finally uncovered and retribution is paid.

10. Roland Barthes, "Littérature objective," *Critique*, X (1954), 581–91.

11. Colette Audry, "La Caméra d'Alain Robbe-Grillet," *La Revue des lettres modernes*, V (1958), 267. "The look which the hero of *Le Voyeur* directs toward the jetty or which the husband of *La Jalousie* casts on his wife's back is unthinking and superficial; it is a dehumanized and desensitized look, pertaining to objects; it is a simple glass lense—one which is purely *objective*."

12. "Notes sur la localisation et les déplacements du point de vue dans la description romanesque," *La Revue des lettres modernes*, V (1958), 258.

13. "Oedipus and Existentialism: *Les Gommes* of Robbe-Grillet," *Wisconsin Studies in Contemporary Literature*, I (1960), 43–74.

14. Alain Robbe-Grillet, as quoted by Bourin in "Techniciens du roman," p. 4.

15. "Littérature objective," p. 582.

16. "The material objects are associated through a kind of indifferent chance," "Littérature littérale," p. 822.

17. "La Subjectivité est la caractéristique du roman contemporain," p. 7.

18. *Le Voyeur* (Paris: Les Editions de Minuit, 1955), p. 39. Future references to this edition appear within the body of the text.

19. "Objects . . . make the crime, they do not explain it: in other words they are literal. Robbe-Grillet's novel remains, therefore, exterior to any psychoanalytic order." "Littérature littérale," p. 823.

20. Claude Mauriac, *L'Alittérature contemporaine* (Paris: Albin Michel, 1958), p. 233.

21. *L'Aurore*, 5 July 1955, as quoted by *Esprit* in "Voici dix romanciers. . . ." (July–August 1958), p. 28.

22. *L'Alittérature contemporaine*, p. 237.

23. "Nouveau Réalisme?" *La NEF*, XV (1958), 67.

24. *NNRF*, July 1955, as quoted by *Esprit* in "Voici dix romanciers. . . . ," p. 28.

25. "La Caméra d'Alain Robbe-Grillet," p. 262.

26. "Plan du labyrinthe de Robbe-Grillet," *Les Temps modernes*, XVI (1960), 158.

27. *Cahiers du Sud*, July 1955, as quoted by *Esprit* in "Voici dix romanciers. . . . ," p. 27.

28. "Description et infraconscience chez Alain Robbe-Grillet," *NRF*, VIII (1960), 890–900.

29. Bruce Morrissette, "Vers une écriture objective: 'Le Voyeur' de Robbe-Grillet," *Saggi e ricerche di letteratura francese* (Milan: Feltrinelli, 1961), pp. 267–98. See also Hazel E. Barnes, "The Ins and Outs of Alain Robbe-Grillett," *Chicago Review*, XV (1962), 21–43.

30. Though in her article on "Jalousie: New Blinds or Old," *Yale French Studies*, no. 24, p. 90, Germaine Brée says that "*Jalousie* appears to be a strictly controlled form of the traditional 'psychological novel.' " Bruce Morrissette, in an article on "La Jalousie" in *Critique*, July 1959, demonstrates most conclusively that this novel is "subjective" and that it is, as Germaine Brée states, a variant of the traditional French psychological novel. These two critics, by stressing the significance of image patterns and recurrent associations in *La Jalousie*, have anticipated the general lines of my own analysis for *Le Voyeur*.

31. One of the most recent critics to acknowledge this "subjectivity," *à propos* of *L'Année dernière à Marienbad*, is Claude Ollier in the October 1961 issue of the *NRF*. This work, says Ollier, "sets out to reconstruct . . . the reality of the mental process, the truth of its genesis and of its becoming, or, as André Breton used to say, 'le fonctionnement réel de la pensée'." See also Yvonne Guers, "La Technique romanesque chez Alain Robbe-Grillet," *FR*, XXXV (1962), 570–77.

32. "Une Voie pour le roman future," *NNRF* (July 1956), pp. 80–81.

33. Faulkner's novels are one of the strongest literary influences on Robbe-Grillet. *The Sound and the Fury*, for

instance, begins with Benjy watching golfers through a fence. The reader does not know, and he cannot know, upon first reading, that hitting golf balls, and Benjy's fascination with the activity of hitting, correspond to his castration and to his point of view. The second paragraph of *Le Voyeur* is, similarly, a capsule summary of Robbe-Grillet's own novel—full of sound and fury, signifying nothing. The dislocations in chronology correspond to analogous shifts in time in *Absalom, Absalom!* Mathias, in *Le Voyeur*, like Ulysses, finds himself one morning on an island. Later in the day, after he has hurled Jacqueline into the ocean, the islanders allude to a mythological monster which comes out of the sea to devour a young girl. The Greek theme is less persistent and less obvious in *Le Voyeur* than in *Les Gommes*, in which, in addition to Faulkner's, we sense a Joycean influence. The presence of this theme in the first two novels (as Morrissette's Oedipal interpretation of *Les Gommes* reveals) suggests a modern mythological context. The sea-monster therefore seems to be Mathias' subconscious compulsive drive. It will be his "siren." Reference to the myth generalizes Mathias' sexuality. By giving us the total picture of one man's psyche and by universalizing it Robbe-Grillet, like Joyce, has re-created a segment of the subconscious of his race.

34. "Plan du Labyrinthe de Robbe-Grillet," p. 159.

35. "Le Réalisme, la psychologie et l'avenir du roman," *Critique*, XIV (1956), 701.

36. "Vers une écriture objective: 'Le Voyeur' de Robbe-Grillet," p. 293.

37. "In Search of the Pure Récit," p. 338.

4—The Gum Erasers: *Oedipus the Detective*

1. *Les Gommes* (Paris: Editions de Minuit, 1953).

2. I am indebted in this study to an article by Bruce Morrissette, "Oedipus and Existentialism: *Les Gommes* of Robbe-Grillet," *Wisconsin Studies in Contemporary Literature*, I (1960), 43–73.

3. "The Guilty Vicarage," *Harper's* (May 1948), p. 407.

4. *Les Gommes*, p. 13. Subsequent page references appear within the body of the text.

5. William Faulkner, *The Sound and the Fury* (New York: Modern Library, 1946), p. 104.

6. *The Anatomy of Criticism* (Princeton University Press, 1957).

7. See Bruno Hahn, "Plan du labyrinthe de Robbe-Grillet," *Les Temps Modernes*, XVI (1960), 150–68. In this article Bruno Hahn discusses, among other things, the subjectivity, the relativity, and the multiplicity of point of view in Robbe-Grillet's novels, the relationship of point of view to error, and the subsequent lack of "communication" between people.

5—In the Labyrinth

1. Alain Robbe-Grillet, *Dans le labyrinthe* (Paris: Editions de Minuit, 1959), pp. 22–23. Future page references to this edition appear within the body of the text.

2. Alain Robbe-Grillet, "Le Réalisme, la psychologie et l'avenir du roman," *Critique*, XII (1956), 701.

3. As quoted by Bruno Hahn, "Plan du Labyrinthe," *Les Temps Modernes*, XVI (1960), 164.

4. "The Ins and Outs of Alain Robbe-Grillet," *Chicago Review*, XV (1962), 43.

5. "Plan du Labyrinthe," p. 164.

6. "La Technique Romanesque chez Alain Robbe-Grillet," *The French Review*, XXXV (1962), 579.

7. Jean-Paul Sartre, *La Nausée* (Paris: Gallimard, 1938), p. 189.

8. Wayne C. Booth, *The Rhetoric of Fiction* (University of Chicago Press, 1961), pp. 384–85.

9. Georges Poulet, *Studies in Human Time*, trans. from the French by Elliott Coleman (New York: Harper & Brothers, 1959), p. 35.

10. Jorge Luis Borges, *Labyrinths* (New York: New Directions, 1962), p. 25.

11. *Labyrinths*, p. xi.

12. *James Joyce*, French trans. by Claude Ternaud (Paris: Robert Marin, 1950), p. 240.

13. James Joyce, *Finnegans Wake*, French trans. of selected passages by André du Bouchet, Introduction by Michel Butor (Paris: Gallimard, 1962), p. 17.

14. Edgar Allan Poe, *Prose Works* (Boston: Riverside Press, 1882–98), IV, 209.

15. "Dans le labyrinthe," *NRF*, no. 85 (1960), 113.

6—This Year at Marienbad—*Film or Novel*

1. Penelope Houston, "L'Année dernière à Marienbad," *Sight and Sound* (Winter 1961/62), p. 26.

2. Alain Robbe-Grillet, "Une Voie pour le roman futur," *NNRF*, IV (1956), 81.

3. Sergei Eisenstein, *The Film Sense*, trans. by Jay Leyda (New York: Meridian, 1959), p. 32.

4. *The Film Sense*, p. 33.

5. *Time* (15 September 1961), p. 76.

6. George Bluestone, *Novels Into Film* (Berkeley: University of California Press, 1961), p. 62.

7. "Last Year at Marienbad," *Show* (March 1962), p. 32.

8. See Preface to *L'Année dernière à Marienbad* (Paris, Editions de Minuit: 1961), p. 12.

9. The plot of *L'Immortelle* is briefly as follows: A French professor, N., arrives in Istanbul where he meets a young lady, Λ., by the Bosphorus. She shows him the city but disappears before he can find out who she is. The professor is advised not to look for her but, disregarding the warning, he searches everywhere and finally finds her in the native quarter in a white Buick. She feels herself spied on continuously by a man with black glasses who holds two mastiffs on a leash. While N. and A. are riding through the city the car skids across the road and A. is killed. One of the mastiffs is heard barking nearby. N. continues his search in an attempt to find out who this mysterious woman is, but the second mastiff appears and

N. dies. The actors are Françoise Brion and her husband Jacques Doniol-Valcroze.

10. See the interesting issue of the *Revue des Lettres Modernes* entitled "Cinéma et Roman," Summer 1958; also Bruce Morrissette, "Roman et Cinéma: Le Cas de Robbe-Grillet," *Symposium*, Summer 1961.

11. *Novels Into Film*, p. 62.

12. The term *ante*-novel (not *anti*) can now be applied to Robbe-Grillet and a few other writers like Daniel Castelain. Castelain's novel *Une Rencontre improbable* (*An Improbable Encounter*) is an exploration of further possibilities inherent in this domain.

13. Jean-Paul Sartre, "American Novelists in French Eyes," *The Atlantic Monthly* (August 1946), pp. 114–118.

14. Michel Mourlet, "Cinéma contre roman," *La Revue des Lettres Modernes*, V (1958), 157.

15. See "La Caméra d'Alain Robbe-Grillet," *La Revue des Lettres Modernes*, V (1958), 267; also "Roman et Cinéma: Le Cas de Robbe-Grillet," *Symposium* (Summer 1961), p. 99.

16. Sigmund Freud, "The Dream Work," as quoted by *Film Culture*, no. 21 (1950), 40.

17. This will in no way resemble the color atrocities perpetrated in the filming of *South Pacific*.

18. See Wayne C. Booth, *The Rhetoric of Fiction* (University of Chicago Press, 1961), pp. 384–85.

19. "American Novelists in French Eyes."

20. Ibid., p. 118.

7—Surrealism and Its Image

1. Claude Sarraute, "La Subjectivité est la caractéristique du roman contemporain," *Le Monde* (11–17 May 1961), p. 7.

2. Alain Robbe-Grillet, "Une Voie pour le roman Futur," *NNRF* (July 1956), p. 82.

3. "L'Année dernière à Marienbad," *Réalités*, no. 184 (1961), 98.

4. "La Subjectivité est la caractéristique du roman contemporain," p. 7.

5. Interview with Jacques Brenner, *Arts* (March 1953).

6. Anna Balakian, *Surrealism: The Road to the Absolute* (New York: Noonday, 1959), p. 109.

8—Conclusion

1. André Malraux, *Les Voix du Silence* (Paris: Gallimard, 1951), p. 628.

2. "Le 'Nouveau Roman,'" *Dictionnaire de littérature contemporaine 1900–1962* (Paris: Editions Universitaires, 1962), p. 82.

3. Claude-Edmonde Magny, *L'Age du Roman Américain* (Paris: Editions du Seuil, 1948), pp. 196–244.

4. Epigraph to "Old 'Values' and the New Novel," by Alain Robbe-Grillet ("Nature, Humanism, Tragedy"), trans. from the French by Bruce Morrissette, *Evergreen Review*, III (1959), 98.

BIBLIOGRAPHY

Works by Robbe-Grillet

L'Année dernière à Marienbad. Paris: Les Editions de Minuit, 1961.

"L'Année dernière à Marienbad," *Réalités*, no. 184 (May 1961), 95–98, 111–15.

"L'Année dernière à Marienbad," *Sight and Sound* (Autumn 1961), pp. 177–80.

Dans le labyrinthe. Paris: Les Editions de Minuit, 1959.

"La Défaite de Reichenfels," *NNRF*, VII (September 1959), 385–410.

Les Gommes. Paris: Les Editions de Minuit, 1953.

L'Immortelle. Paris: Les Editions de Minuit, 1963.

Instantanés. Paris: Les Editions de Minuit, 1962.

La Jalousie. Paris: Les Editions de Minuit, 1957.

"Nature, Humanisme, Tragédie," *NNRF*, (October 1958), pp. 580–605.

"Notes sur la localisation et les déplacements du point de vue dans la description romanesque," *La Revue des Lettres Modernes*, V (Summer 1958), 256–59.

"Le 'Nouveau Roman'," *Dictionnaire de littérature contemporaine 1900–1962*. Paris: Editions Universitaires, 1962, pp. 75–83.

"Nouveau Roman—Homme Nouveau," *La Revue de Paris*, no. 68 (September 1961), pp. 115–21.

"Old 'Values' and the New Novel" (translated from French by Bruce Morrissette), *Evergreen Review*, no. 9 (Summer 1959), 98–119.

"Le Réalisme, la psychologie et l'avenir du roman," *Critique*, XII (July 1956), 694–701.

"Une Voie pour le roman futur," *NNRF*, IV (July 1956), 77–84.

Le Voyeur. Paris: Les Editions de Minuit, 1955.

Selected Robbe-Grillet Criticism

Alter, Jean. "The Treatment of Time in Alain Robbe-Grillet's *La Jalousie*," *C.L.A. Journal*, III (1959), 46–55.

Anonymous. "All Things to All Men," *Time* (16 March 1962), p. 56.

———. "Last Year at Marienbad," *Show*, (March 1962), p. 32.

———. "Movies Abroad—The Top Drop," *Time* (15 September 1961), p. 76.

———. "The Neo-Realists," *Time* (July 20, 1962), pp. 80–81.

Audry, Colette. "La Caméra d'Alain Robbe-Grillet," *La Revue des Lettres* Modernes, V (1958), 259–69.

Barnes, Hazel. "The Ins and Outs of Alain Robbe-Grillet," *Chicago Review*, XV (Winter-Spring 1962), 21–43.

Barthes, Roland. "Littérature littérale," *Critique*, XII (1955), 820–26.

———. "Littérature objective," *Critique*, X (July–August 1954), 581–91.

Berger, Yves. "Dans le labyrinthe," *NRF*, VIII (January 1960), 113.

Bourdet, Denise. "Le Cas Robbe-Grillet," *La Revue de Paris*, LXVI (1959), 130–35.

Bourin, André. "Techniciens du roman," *Nouvelles Littéraires*, (22 January 1955), 1, 4.

Brée, Germaine. "New Blinds or Old," *Yale French Studies*, no. 24 (Summer 1959), 87–91.

Champigny, Robert. "In Search of the Pure Récit," *The American Society Legion of Honor Magazine*," XXVII (Winter 1956/57), 331–42.

Dort, Bernard. "Are These Novels 'Innocent', " *Yale French Studies*, no. 24 (Summer 1959), 22–30.

———. "Des Romans 'innocents'?" *Esprit*, no. 7–8 (July–August 1958), 100–110.

———. "Sur 'l'espace', " *Esprit* (July–August 1958), pp. 77–83.

Dreyfus, Dina. "De l'ascétisme dans le roman," *Esprit* (July–August 1958), pp. 60–67.

Erval, François. "Romans—*Dans le labyrinthe* par Alain Robbe-Grillet," *L'Express* (1 October 1959), pp. 32–33.

Estang, Luc. "Lettre à un jeune romancier," *Esprit* (July–August 1958), pp. 111–20.

Girard, René. "Pride and Passion in the Contemporary Novel," *Yale French Studies*, no. 24 (Summer 1959), 3–11.

Giraud, Raymond. "Unrevolt Among the Unwriters in France Today," *Yale French Studies*, no. 24 (Summer 1959), 11–18.

Grenier, Cynthia. "Alain Resnais of France—Explorations in the Unconscious," *Saturday Review* (23 December 1961), pp. 37–38.

Guers, Yvonne. "La Technique Romanesque chez Alain Robbe-Grillet," *The French Review*, XXXV (May 1962), 570–77.

Hahn, Bruno. "Plan du Labyrinthe," *Les Temps Modernes*, XVI (1960), 164.

Houston, Penelope. "L'Année dernière à Marienbad," *Sight and Sound* (Winter 1961/1962), pp. 26–28.

Howlett, Jacques. "Distance et Personne dans quelques romans d'ajourd'hui," *Esprit* (July–August 1958), pp. 87–91.

———. "Notes sur l'objet dans le roman," *Esprit* (July–August 1958), pp. 67–72.

Kauffmann, Stanley. "Room With a Déjà Vu," *Show* (May 1962), pp. 30–32.

Lagrolet, Jean. "Nouveau Réalisme?" *La NEF*, XV (1958), 62–70.

LeSage, Laurent. *The French New Novel*. University Park, Penn.: The Pennsylvania State University Press, 1962.

Loy, J. Robert. "Things in Recent French Literature," *PMLA*, vol. 71 (March 1956), 27–41.

Magny, Olivier de. "Panorama d'une nouvelle littérature romanesque," *Esprit*, (July–August 1958), pp. 3–18.

Mauriac, Claude. "Alain Robbe-Grillet et le roman futur," *Preuves*, no. 68 (October 1956), 92–96.

———. "The 'New Novel' in France," *New York Times Book Review* (19 June 1960), 5, 12.

Morrissette, Bruce. "The New Novel in France," *Chicago Review*, XV (Winter/Spring 1962), 1–19.

————. "New Structure in the Novel: *Jealousy*, by Alain Robbe-Grillet," *Evergreen Review*, III (1959), 103–7, 164–91.

————. "Oedipus and Existentialism: *Les Gommes* of Robbe-Grillet," *Wisconsin Studies in Contemporary Literature*, I (1960), 43–73.

————. "Roman et Cinéma: Le Cas de Robbe-Grillet," *Symposium* (Summer 1961), pp. 85–104.

————. *Les Romans de Robbe-Grillet*. Paris: Les Editions de Minuit, 1963.

————. "Surfaces et structures dans les romans de Robbe-Grillet," *The French Review*, XXXI (April 1958), 364–70.

————. "Vers une écriture objective: 'Le Voyeur' de Robbe-Grillet," *Saggi e ricerche di letteratura francese*. Milan: Feltrinelli, 1961, pp. 267–98.

Mourlet, Michel. "Cinéma contre roman," *La Revue des Lettres Modernes*, V (1958), 157.

Ollier, Claude. "Ce Soir à Marienbad," *NAF*, IX (October 1961), 711–20.

Peyre, Henri. "Trends in the Contemporary French Novel," *New French Writing*. New York: Grove Press, 1961, pp. 73–88.

Pinguad, Bernard. "L'Ecole du refus," *Esprit* (July–August 1958), pp. 55–60.

————. "Je, Vous, Il," *Esprit* (July–August 1958), pp. 91–100.

————. "The School of Refusal," *Yale French Studies*, no. 24 (Summer 1959), 18–22.

————. "Y a-t-il quelqu'un?" *Esprit* (July–August 1958), pp. 83–86.

Ricardou, Jean. "Description et infraconscience chez Alain Robbe-Grillet," *NRF*, VIII (November 1960), 890–900.

Sarraute, Claude. "La Subjectivité est la caractéristique du roman contemporain," *Le Monde* (11–17 May 1961), p. 7.

Special Issues. "Cinéma et Roman," *La Revue des Lettres Modernes*, Summer 1958.

————. "Midnight Novelists and others," *Yale French Studies*, no. 24 (Summer 1959).

————. "Le 'Nouveau Roman'," *Esprit* (July–August 1958).

————. "Le 'Nouveau Roman'," *La Revue des Lettres Modernes* (Forthcoming).

Stoltzfus, Ben. "A Novel of Objective Subjectivity: *Le Voyeur* by Alain Robbe-Grillet," *PMLA*, vol. 77 (September 1962), 499–508.

Weiner, Seymour S. "A Look at Techniques and Meaning in Robbe-Grillet's *Voyeur*," *Modern Language Quarterly*, no. 3 (September 1962), 217–25.

INDEX

A la recherche du temps
perdu, 115. See also
Proust, Marcel
Absalom, Absalom!, 13, 149.
See also Faulkner, William
Adam, 138
Adolphe, 45, 118. See also
Constant, Benjamin
L'Age du roman américain,
119. See also Edmonde-
Magny, Claude
Age of suspicion, 5, 9, 45,
46, 64–65, 110. See also
Sarraute, Nathalie
Amerika, 97. See also Kafka,
Franz
Anouilh, Jean, 99
Ante-novel, 152
Anti-novel, 152
Antonioni, Michelangelo, 102
Aragon, Louis, 131
Ariadne, 99
Aristotelian tragedy, 69
As I Lay Dying, 80. See also
Faulkner, William
Au château d'Argol, 91. See
also Gracq, Julien
Auden, W. H., 69
Audry, Colette, 46, 55, 111
Autant-Laura, Claude, 115

Balakian, Anna, 134
Balzac, Honoré de, 5, 7, 14,
21, 27, 51, 104, 138
Barnes, Hazel, 56, 85
Baroncelli, Jean de, 102
Barthes, Roland, 43, 46, 47,
54, 55, 102, 144
Bateau Ivre, 128. See also
Rimbaud, Arthur
Baudelaire, Charles, 40
Beach, Joseph, W., 9
Beauvoir, Simone de, 119
Beckett, Samuel, 3, 4, 30,
87, 94, 137
Berger, Yves, 97
Bergman, Ingmar, 102
Bergson, Henri, 37
Blanchot, Maurice, 55
Bluestone, George, 103, 107,
109
Booth, Wayne C., 150
Borges, Jorge Luis, 26, 93–94
Bourdet, Denise, 42, 146
Bourin, André, 146
Brée, Germaine, 55, 148
Brenner, Jacques, 42, 153
Breton, André, 124, 126–27,
129–30, 132, 133
Brion, Françoise, 152
Bruegel, Pieter (the elder),
89
Butor, Michel, 3, 5, 12–13,
46, 73, 86, 119, 138–40,
142–44
—L'Emploi du temps, 13,
73, 86, 87, 89, 138, 142–
43; Modification, La, 12;
Répertoire, 5

Cain and Abel, 89
Caldwell, Erskine, 118
Caligula, 19, 40. See also Ca-
mus, Albert

L'Etranger, 7–8, 16–27, 30, 55, 80, 118–19, 137. *See also* Camus, Albert

L'Etre et le néant, 30. *See also* Sartre, Jean-Paul

Existentialism: 3, 15, 135–36; and "dreadful freedom," 40; premises and themes, 87; despair and new morality, 88. *See also* Sartre, Jean-Paul

Fall, The, 86. *See also* Camus, Albert

Faulkner, William: 3, 13, 45, 51, 53, 74, 78, 80, 110, 119–20, 149; influence of, 23, 47, 67–69, 118–20; and tragedy, 138

Faustism, 137

Faux-Monnayeurs, Les, 79. *See also* Gide, André

Fielding, Henry, 6, 7

Finnegans Wake, 94–95, 141. *See also* Joyce, James

Flaubert, Gustave: 5, 10, 49, 51–54, 89–90, 117; influence of, 22–23, 48, 138–39; and God, 51; "transitions savantes," 52; as objective novelist, 110

Freud, Sigmund: 5, 49, 114–15, 120, 134; and determinism, 42, 64, 123; and free association, 43; influence of, 73; influence on surrealism, 126

Friedman, Norman, 6, 9

Frye, Northrop, 80

"Garden of Forking Paths, The," 93. *See also* Borges, Jorge Luis

Gide, André, 79, 80, 118, 120, 139

Giraudoux, Jean, 99

God: existential view of, 40; revolt against, 138

Gracq, Julien, 91

Green, Julien, 24, 43, 44

Guers, Yvonne, 86

Guicharnaud, Jacques, 15

Hahn, Bruno, 55, 85, 86, 150

Hardy, Thomas: 7, 12, 14, 33, 37; and anthropomorphism, 70, 141. *See also* "new novel"

Hawthorne, Nathaniel, 94

Hegel, George Wilhelm Friedrich, 134

Hemingway, Ernest: 25, 110, 115, 118, 120; influence on "new novel," 47

L'Herbe, 12, 14, 119. *See also* Simon, Claude

Hiroshima mon amour, 103, 117. *See also* Duras, Marguerite and Resnais, Alain

Hitchcock, Alfred, 81

Hoffman, Frederick J., 4

"l'homme engagé," prototype of, 86. *See also* existentialism

Houston, Penelope, 103

Hugo, Victor, 53

Husserl, Edmund, influence of, 15, 39

I Am a Camera, 39. *See also* Isherwood, Christopher

Ideal essense, 39. *See also* Plato

L'Immoraliste, 139. *See also* Gide, André

Isherwood, Christopher, 39

James, Henry, 3, 8, 15, 53, 80, 110, 120

Joyce, James: 3, 4, 5, 10, 13, 53, 109–10, 119, 137, 141–43; influence of, 23, 94–95